The No-Nonsense Guide to Archives and Re

Margaret Crockett

facet publishing

Published by Facet Publishing
7 Ridgmount Street, London WC1E 7AE
www.facetpublishing.co.uk

Facet Publishing is wholly owned by CILIP: the Chartered Institute of Library and Information Professionals.

British Library Cataloguing in Publication Data
A catalogue record for this book is available from the British Library.

ISBN 978-1-85604-855-2

First published 2016

Text printed on FSC accredited material.

Typeset from author's files in 10/13 pt Palatino Linotype and Myriad Pro by Facet Publishing Production.
Printed and made in Great Britain by CPI Group (UK) Ltd, Croydon, CR0 4YY.

Contents

List of figures, tables and checklists

Figures

Tables

Checklists

Acknowledgements

This book has been a long time in the writing and I would like to express my gratitude to all of my colleagues, friends and family who have supported and encouraged me through the process. In particular I want to acknowledge and thank Janet Foster, friend and colleague, always on my side, whose influence on my career has been incalculable both as a role model and a fellow explorer in the uncharted territory of our common training and consulting enterprise. Without Janet and the Archive-Skills Consultancy the book would not be what it is. The team at Facet deserve thanks for seeing the possibility of such a book with me as the author, and guiding me through the whole production. My thanks to Alex Abraham and Jenny Crockett who acted as lay readers, commenting on the first chapter, and to Karen Anderson, who was generous in sharing her own editorial experience. I am also very grateful to Emilie Gagnet Leumas, who gallantly volunteered to act as my peer reader at short notice and to a tight deadline. Her comments and copy-editing represent a marked improvement to the finished work. Finally, thanks go to my husband, Iain Brown, for his nicely judged advice (never too much) drawn from a previous life in publishing, for indexing this book and for his understanding, patience and encouragement.

Margaret Crockett

Introduction

This book is written for all those working in archives and records management, especially those without formal training, but also people managing archives and records management staff and those working closely with archives and records management, such as IT professionals, librarians and museum curators. It is intended as a practical how-to-do-it guide to managing archives and records and covers all aspects of recordkeeping and archives management following the records' journey through the lifecycle. Because of this, the chapters are not of equal length, but divide into the four main work areas: current records; records management; archives management; and archives preservation. The book deals with records and archives in all formats and unless specifically mentioned as paper or digital, the guidance is format-neutral. Reference to 'corporate' records is not intended in the narrow private enterprise sense, but rather the more general 'body corporate'. Similarly when 'business' is mentioned, it is in the sense of the wider work and goals of any organization.

CHAPTER 1

Concepts and context

Archives and records: concepts and terminology

For those of us concerned with managing records and archives it is of paramount importance that we can articulate and advocate exactly what it is that we are looking after. Before discussing how to manage them, let's agree working definitions for the material itself.

Records

First of all, let's look at the term 'record'. Records and archives are inextricably linked, which is why this book covers both records and archives management as one holistic discipline. We need to understand what records are in order to define archives. Records consist of recorded information which provides evidence of decisions, planning processes, financial transactions, agreements – in fact pretty much any human activity. Records can be in any medium or format.

Records usually arise as a by-product of business or social activity: for example the invoice for consulting services is part of the process of letting the client know how much they have to pay on the fulfilment of a contractual (written or verbal) agreement. It is rare for records to be deliberately created for their own sake, although there are exceptions. For example, medieval chronicles, personal diaries or letters can be written with the intent of recording the author's or the author's sponsor's viewpoint.

> **Record:** recorded information in any media or format, providing reliable evidence of human activity.

Records also need to have certain characteristics or features in order to be 'good' records that we can trust and depend on. It is important to know the creator of the record. If the record does not stand alone, it is important to have the links to the other records that together form the comprehensive record. These links and the author provide the context of the record, which in turn allows us to be confident about its authenticity. We also like to be sure that the record has not been tampered with. These characteristics depend upon a variety of things, including:

- the custody of the record(s) over time
- inherent indications in the physical record, such as inconsistencies in script, the physical carrier or the way it is set out
- discrepancies in the audit trail or metadata of digital records.

Figure 1.1 gives some tips on how to assess the authenticity of records.

There is no way to realistically enforce rules on creating records to ensure that they are trustworthy; however, some things to look out for which help to indicate the reliability of records include:

- evidence of the author – we recognize the handwriting perhaps, or know what organization it has come from because of the headed paper or domain name or because it is bound in with or filed with other records in the series, clearly indicating the creator
- the record is complete and final
- with legal records, they are signed, sealed or have a format we recognize and are written by or drawn up by solicitors
- there is a date and/or a serial number to show the record's context.

Figure 1.1 *How can we trust that records are authentic?*

Record series: a group of records that support a specific work responsibility, for example a volume of board minutes or set of social worker's case files, each pertaining to a different instance of the same activity.

In fact, sometimes recorded information may not be a record at all. For instance, an old family photograph without any information about who is portrayed is not a record of anything. However, the school trophy cup engraved with winners of the annual 100-metre sprint does provide evidence of successive victors over time. Good questions to ask are: 'What is this a record of?', 'Is it the original?' and 'Is it evidence of the organization's work?'

With the advent of computers and recorded information in digital format, archives and records management professionals have had to reconsider many of the principles that guided their work for decades. It can be difficult to establish the authenticity of digital records because the author is not always clearly identified. Drafts and versions may not be clearly numbered, so that we might not be sure we have the definitive record. Digital records are easily copied and copies are indistinguishable from the 'original', and so we question which instance is the master. Before computers the fact that records could not be changed was considered to be an essential quality of a reliable record. But we need to change digital records in order to preserve them, not to mention the fact that opening them on different machines in different systems (in the case of e-mail, for example) can change the file format. These are all challenges that have yet to be definitively met and solved. The processes for creating, handling, transmitting and preserving digital records to ensure their authenticity and render them reliable over time are still evolving. However, it is already clear that we need to ensure that certain characteristics are embedded in digital records at the point of creation and need to be considered even before a new computer system is designed, specified or procured, to ensure they have the necessary functionality to create and maintain reliable records.

Archives

'Archives' is a word that means different things to different people, depending on their professional and personal background (see Figure 1.2). It is important that those of us who look after archives and manage records are clear about what they are and how they are distinct from old books, data or information.

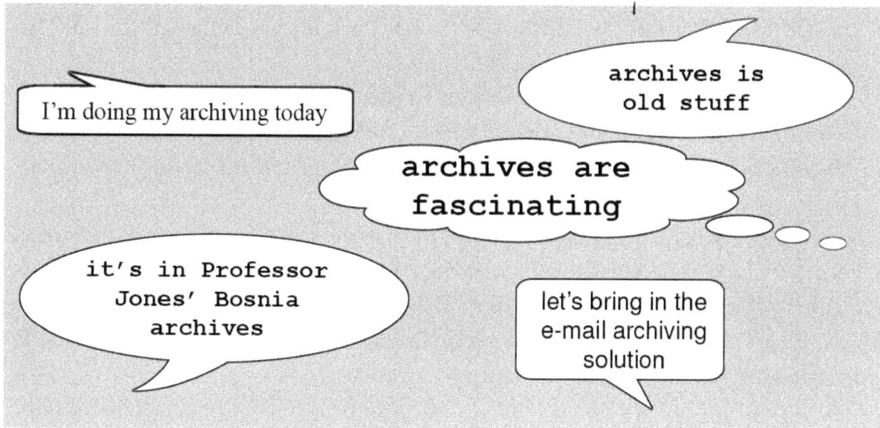

Figure 1.2 *Popular conceptions of archives*

Often people assume that archives have to be old or that they are no longer useful for current work or everyday life. They will often consider that they are about a subject. They might say they are historical, interesting, important and/or authoritative. Organizations sometimes have an e-mail archiving feature whereby the e-mail gets regularly moved to a different storage area. We often hear people say they are going to do their 'archiving', which means moving older files to storage which is not so accessible.

Whatever ideas you have come up with about archives, they will all be valid and probably most will chime in some way with the concepts that archives professionals keep in mind when taking in, processing and making archives accessible, such as these:

- Archives are records which document the history of organizations, individuals and families.
- They are the primary source, the first hand, contemporary account of what happened.
- They are not just a random collection, but are usually created and received by organizations, individuals or families in the course of business, activities and living.
- All the records in an archive will have been created by the same organization, family or individual, they have the same origin and context.
- Archives are unique (unlike museum objects or books) – there is only one record of an event or decision (even if it consists of different accounts from different sources).
- Archives may be old but archival value does not depend upon age, rather upon the informational and evidential value of the content.
- Archives are selected from the body of records to provide a lasting resource for the history of the family, person or organization that created the archive; they are information-rich and generally provide all the evidence required for the creator's story.
- Not all records are archives: we can't keep every record; some records do not add anything significant to the story; we keep the records which together give the most complete picture of the creator's history.

Archives are therefore the raw material of history; they provide the first-hand account and evidence of the story of the individual(s) or organization. They are selected because they document the key activity without unnecessary detail. It can also be helpful to see records and archives as arising organically from the activity of the creating entity.

> **Archive:** records of one organization, family or individual, selected for permanent preservation because they provide key evidence of the entity's history.

So when people talk about 'doing the archiving' or 'keeping things in the archive', generally there has been no assessment of the historical significance of the records; they have just been moved because the space they occupy is needed for something else (usually for more current records). Published information is not archival because it is not unique and is generally not a primary source providing first-hand evidence. However, publications (including things like annual reports, catalogues of products, anniversary souvenirs) from the creator of the archives are archival, because they are a record of information that the organization felt it important to circulate widely.

> **Provenance:** the archive's creator, be it an individual, family or organization – essentially tells us where the archive came from.

Within an archive, the sub-creators are important, too. The records produced by the accounts department or Great-Uncle William need to be identified and kept separate from those of the marketing department or Granny Mills. Knowing about the relationships between the records and the different parts of the organization, family or the individual's life allows us to identify the separate record groups and understand how they relate to each other. Similarly, the various groups taken together provide more complete evidence and information about the creating entity than any single record, or group, could do in isolation. We should note that users may not be interested in the records in context but respecting the origins and context of the records ensures that their authenticity and reliability are maintained. Archivists also refer to the entirety of records from one provenance as 'fonds', from the French, meaning 'root' or 'origin'. This word allows us to distinguish a single archive from the archive repository and its collective holdings.

Remember, records from a variety of different organizations that have been brought together by an individual or organization in pursuit of research interests, or to satisfy collecting interests, do not form an archive in the strict sense that the records come from the same creator. We should never mix archives of different creators, for example, in a subject-based structure, because we would lose both evidential value and context. However, sometimes an archive is formed because a collector has gathered archival material, perhaps with research notes and copies of published works and/or records, and organized it into his or her own filing system. This would then be regarded as the archive of that collector. Unfortunately, the principle of not mixing archives of different creators is confused by the fact that we also call the building where the archives are kept an archive (let's call it the archive repository) and the repository might house multiple archives with different provenances.

> **Original order:** the organization of archival records as they were when last used by the creating entity.

A final point to make about archives is that the links between records within the archives are important. These links, and the way the individual records were organized and related to each other when created and used by the creating entity, need to be maintained and documented, because they form part of the authenticity and credibility of the archive. They also usually reflect activities and functions. We should not, and indeed do not need to, devise or make up a suitable organization for the archives. Rather, we seek to identify the original order in which the archives were organized when the records were current.

The difference between records and archives: although all archives are records, not all records are archives. Records are the greater group of primary source material from which archives are selected.

Record media and formats

We have to manage all records and archives, regardless of their media or format. Let's identify and define the common record media and formats.

Media

Medium: the physical carrier of the record.

It is important to note that the record medium does not have a bearing on whether it is a record or not. For example, a record can be a roll of parchment, a bound volume or a set of web pages.

Thinking about records in context, the archives of a person or organization may include paper records, computer records and/or audiovisual materials such as film or photographs. Even record series themselves may contain records in different formats; for example, a correspondence series may start off as letters written on paper and then become e-mail held on computer.

Archives can be found on the following kinds of media:

- paper
- parchment
- wood (e.g., tally sticks)
- stone (e.g., gravestones)
- photographic prints
- photographic slides
- glass plate negatives
- silent/audio film
- magnetic film
- compact, hard or floppy disks.

This list is not comprehensive and we can reasonably expect it to be ever-growing! You may also be wondering about records that are 'in the cloud', which will probably be on servers managed by the cloud computing service provider, depending on the communication or storage solution used. Servers are, of course, hard drives.

Format

> **Format:** 1. (Physical) construction of a record. 2. (Intellectual) characteristics of a record. 3. (Digital) layout of data according to program type.

If the medium is the physical carrier, then the format is the way the information or data is arranged within or on the carrier. It may be the physical construction of the record, for example a bound volume or a ring binder. It may be the intellectual characteristics of the record, for example diaries or registers, where content usually follows a set pattern. With digital records it will refer to the organization of the data itself such that the program will be able to recognize, read and display it – we are all familiar with formats such as Microsoft Word, Open Office and rich text format. Table 1.1 gives examples of different formats for various types of media.

Table 1.1 *Media and formats*

<table>
<tr><th>Medium</th><th>Examples of formats</th></tr>
<tr><td>Paper</td><td>• bound volume
• file with treasury tag
• ring binder
• bundle of folded documents
• deeds
• diaries</td></tr>
<tr><td>Wood</td><td>• tally sticks</td></tr>
<tr><td>Parchment</td><td>• roll
• chronicles
• deeds
• laws</td></tr>
<tr><td>Stone</td><td>• gravestones
• memorial stones</td></tr>
<tr><td>Photographic prints</td><td>• black-and-white
• colour
• 3″ x 5″
• contact prints</td></tr>
<tr><td>Photographic transparency</td><td>• plastic slide</td></tr>
<tr><td>Glass plate negatives</td><td>• collodion wet plate negative
• gelatin dry plate</td></tr>
<tr><td>Movie film</td><td>• 35 mm film
• 3D film</td></tr>
<tr><td>Magnetic film</td><td>• 16 mm
• super 8</td></tr>
<tr><td>Compact disk</td><td rowspan="3">• Microsoft Office programmes (MS Word, Excel, PowerPoint, etc.)
• e-mail browsers
• internet browsers
• databases</td></tr>
<tr><td>Hard disk drive</td></tr>
<tr><td>Floppy disk</td></tr>
</table>

Types of archive repository

There are many different kinds of archive repositories and this section is intended to introduce you to the main kinds of archive institutions found in the UK, but also with reference to what there is in other countries. UK archive repositories – or rather their contents – reflect the age and diversity of culture, communities and individuals that have lived in the British Isles since the Middle Ages. These archives include the records of national and local government, the established and non-conformist churches, universities and guilds or professional associations, schools, hospitals, museums, charities, landed estates, businesses, social clubs and societies, not forgetting individuals and families. In fact any kind of organization or activity that results in records or documentation can probably be found in an archive somewhere.

To give a more concrete idea of the extent of archives in the UK, *British Archives: a guide to archive resources in the UK*, by Janet Foster and Julia Sheppard (Palgrave, 4th edition, 2001) contains 1231 entries giving details of places holding records which, in some way, are made available to the public. The ARCHON Directory[1] hosted by The National Archives contains more up-to-date but less detailed information on British archives. In June 2015 it contained over 2500 entries. The aim of this introductory chapter is to give an overview of the breadth and depth of records and archives and their role in society.

National archives

Most countries have a national archive institution which takes in and looks after the records of central government. However, their mandates and resources vary greatly. The French national archives, or *Les Archives Nationales*, established in September 1790, was the earliest national archives institution of this type. A law dating from 1794 sets out three principles, which still guide French national archival management:

1 The national archives are managed from the centre.
2 There is free public access.
3 There should be a national network of archives (realized as an archives service in every French *département*).

In the UK the Public Record Office (PRO) was established in 1838 to 'keep safely the public records', but the remit for provision of access to the public was less clear and there was no mandate to control a network of local government archives in the way the Archives Nationales does in France. Since 1838 the nature and role of the Public Record Office has evolved, with the authority of a series of Public Records Acts, to include the provision of free public access (both in the sense that the holdings are generally open and there is no charge to view records on site). In 2003 the PRO changed its name to The National Archives (TNA).

Some national archives (such as Canada, Ethiopia and Iraq) have been merged with the national library, to form a joint agency for archives and bibliographic material.

Holdings

National archives hold the records of central government; however, the exact composition of the holdings of a national archives will depend on its legislative or regulatory mandate and the history of the country and nation, in accordance with its collecting policy.

In countries where there is a long history of centralized government, holdings will include the records of departments which no longer exist because of reorganization. Holdings might also include the records of former companies that were nationalized: a UK example is the records of the Great Northern Railway Company, which became part of British Rail. Similarly, national archives might hold records of government entities that have been privatized, another UK example being the records of the British Railways Board, now British Railways (known as British Rail).

Where the government has its roots in a monarchical government, the national archives would also include the records of the royal family, particularly those records relating to the management of its possessions and estates, including the country or countries the monarchs ruled.

Depending on the mandate of the national archives, its holdings might include the records of individuals or organizations of national significance. Some national archives hold ecclesiastical, court and school records. With the advent of digital records, national archives may also hold large datasets emerging from government surveys or even academic research.

Services

The responsibilities of and services offered by national archives will vary according to legislative and cultural context, but all national archives will be taking in records, cataloguing them and storing them in the best possible physical environment to ensure future preservation and access. Most national archives will provide on-site access to the archive material by the public and also probably a range of research services at a distance, for example a copying service and answering enquiries about the holdings.

Some national archives have a remit to supervise or manage a network of local government or decentralized government archives around the country – this can even extend to the archives of all public bodies, such as universities and schools.

National archives are also usually concerned about records management practices within the departments and other public bodies whose records they receive. Again, depending on their mandate, they will offer guidance or issue instructions for records management to ensure that the quality and organization of the archives is good at the point of transfer to the national archives.

Sometimes the national archives will be responsible for related government functions which are not strictly speaking archival. This might include keeping registers of private records and archives of national significance of which it does not have custody, acting as ombudsman for access to information legislation or running the government's publishing operation.

Mission

Again, the national archives' mission will vary according to the legal and cultural context of the country but the aims of the national archives might include:

- protecting and safeguarding government archives for use by future generations
- providing access facilities and information to support the use of the records
- ensuring accountability and transparency through the provision of records management policy and guidance
- ensuring that the documentary evidence in the archives represents the 'story' of the nation.

Apart from taking in and looking after the records of UK government as explained above, TNA also takes responsibility for assisting government departments in managing their current records. Their explicit powers in this respect are limited but they offer guidance and, as the records become less current and closer to the 20-year deadline when they must be deposited in TNA, TNA staff become more proactive in setting out requirements for record selection and the provision of record inventories.

TNA incorporates the Office of Public Sector Information, which is responsible for policy, standards, and supporting the re-use of public sector information in accordance with UK law and EU Directives. Her Majesty's Stationery Office, responsible for publishing UK Acts of Parliament and other official information, is also part of TNA.

The Historical Manuscripts Commission forms part of TNA. It carries out a function established by Royal Warrant to gather information on privately held archives and to provide advice to owners. However, unlike many national archive institutions, TNA generally does not take in private archives of national importance.

TNA traditionally had a small inspectorial role with respect to other archive repositories in the UK which was limited to those archives wishing to hold public records of local interest (for example court records). However, this inspection role has evolved such that TNA is now part of a partnership, the Archive Service Accreditation Committee, which has introduced an accreditation scheme setting a standard for the management of archives and offering 'a badge of external recognition and endorsement of [the] service'.[2] This is in accordance with The National Archives' increased and more explicit leadership role in the archives sector in the UK.

A final point to make about the UK national archive situation is that Northern Ireland and Scotland have their own national archives (the National Records of Scotland and the Public Record Office of Northern Ireland respectively) for records of the devolved governments' administration as well as records of the UK government departments pertaining exclusively or mostly to Scotland or Northern Ireland.

State archives

We find state archives in federal states, such as the USA, Australia and Germany (where they are called *Staatsarchiv*). As you might expect, these archival authorities have remits and holdings similar to those of national archives with respect to the records and archives of their governmental responsibilities and jurisdictions. Sometimes the archives authority is also the records management adviser and authority, sometimes it has jurisdiction over local government and advises and/or takes in records of cities and other local territorial archives such as counties. State archives can also be joined with the state library service.

Local government archives

Most UK county, city and borough councils maintain their historical archives, even though the legislative basis for this, the 1972 Local Government Act, is fairly weak. It has quite a lot to say about depositories for community and parish documents and allowing electors to inspect local authority proceedings and accounts, but the concept of an archive to keep historical records does not shine through the difficult legal wording. Local government archive repositories usually take in the records of the authority and its predecessors, including those whose functions are defunct, such as the poor law administration. Local government archives also usually collect the records of local individuals and businesses.

Some UK county and city archives have collections that date back to the Middle Ages and/or include records that are of great significance for the nation's history, such as those documenting the businesses that helped create the industrial revolution, the movements that affected human and civil rights such as the abolition of slavery, and the families and individuals that served in government and the military.

Like national archive repositories, the work of local government archives includes the physical protection of the archive material, the development of catalogues and other finding aids and the provision of access services. Many offer a service to schools and other learning institutions, employing education officers to manage on-site and web-based educational activities and information. Staff in local government archives might also mount exhibitions and produce or commission publications based on the records they hold. Many also encourage and support friends groups, which provide volunteers to work on the collections and/or raise awareness of the archives, as well as funds for projects and other sanctioned purposes. Records management services may be part of the archives service, closely linked to it or totally separate.

In some areas the archives of several neighbouring authorities, or former authorities, have been combined into a joint service. An example of this is the Dorset History Centre and the Joint Archives Service, where the archives service for Poole, Bournemouth and Dorset has been based in the Dorset History Centre in Dorchester since 1991. It is funded and governed jointly by the three authorities.

In other countries the situation is similar, with local archives at different levels depending on the governance structure in place in each particular country. They provide records and archives management services to the parent authority.

Business archives

Business archives are the records of private sector organizations engaged in trade and commerce. However, over time the public/private status of these organizations can change, for example the British railway companies which were nationalized and subsequently privatized, or a company which sets up a trust for philanthropic purposes. All businesses create archival records but not all identify and preserve them as a distinct corporate goal. Some businesses have consciously made the decision to identify and preserve their archival records in-house. Business archives may also be deposited in local, state or national archives, particularly if the company is no longer in business, and some university archives have considerable collections of business records.

There are many notable examples of business or company archives of established and respected commercial organizations. These include archives of the banking, pharmaceutical, retail and oil industries, brewing, publishers, architects, television companies, to name a few. The remit of company archives varies greatly according to the motivation in supporting an archive or to the company's remit. Some companies find their archive has promotional and commercial value, for example the Selfridges archive, which evolved as an archive of the records of the business' promotional and advertising activities. It is used by staff to inspire and support current work from window-dressing to campaigns and in-store exhibitions. It is also used by select researchers from other organizations such as the production company for the *Mr Selfridge* television series. Other companies keep more comprehensive archives as the corporate memory or through pride in a long-standing historical presence.

Company archives may allow external researchers to use their holdings, limit use to internal staff only, or may even carry out research for internal users. Business archives can be kept in storage owned and managed by the company itself or may be contracted out to commercial storage. Older company archives may be deposited in public archives and more recent material held in-house while needed to support current business or remaining commercially sensitive. Business archives may also have a remit for records management.

Schools

In the UK, state-run schools do not usually consciously manage their archives, although certain records must be created and maintained to meet legislation and regulation. Private and independent schools are increasingly investing resources to manage their archives and in the UK and Australia, for example, school archivists form active special-interest groups within the wider profession.

School archives frequently have a slightly wider collecting remit than other archives because they act as a repository for objects such as school uniforms and prizes, as well as books. Apart from the school's institutional records, there are often many small gifts and deposits from ex-pupils and teachers, which can make the archivist's principle of respecting and documenting the separate creators especially time-consuming. However, school archives can provide an invaluable source of materials and inspiration for staff and pupils alike, as well as information and images to support fund-raising and PR for the school.

Family and individuals' archives

People create and keep records of themselves as private individuals, even if some of their activities, such as writing poetry or novels, or renting out property, could be categorized as business activity (and it can be hard to separate the records of the two). The personal, professional and business activities of individuals generate records and papers, which, if the individual is important or famous enough, may be retained in archives. One example is the archives of Winston Churchill. The records generated whilst he was a British government minister will be part of one or other of the public record series in the UK Parliamentary Archives or The National Archives, but his personal papers are held by the Churchill Archives Centre at Churchill College, Cambridge. Other individuals whose records have been judged to be of archival value are represented in collecting archives such as the University of Oxford's Bodleian Library, which holds private papers of politicians, diplomats, journalists, and 'others active in public life'. Some individuals' archives have been deposited in publicly funded repositories according to their collecting policies.

Similarly, families also generate records, although most families have a limited amount, confined usually to the nuclear family or just the couple. However, there are families that possess a business or property, which widens the scope of their records beyond the personal family records to include the records of commerce, ownership, land management and anything else that documents rights, obligations discharged, decisions made or work done. An example of a family archive would be that of the Duke of Northumberland, whose title and property have their roots in the 11th century. The castle at Alnwick has a records tower and the Duke employs an archivist to manage estate, family and business records stretching back 800 years. Access to the records of landed estates is at the discretion of the owner, as is any investment of resources (including the employment of professionals).

Many family archives have been deposited in public archive repositories and will be subject to the access policy. Wherever they are held, these records document aspects of history and society that are not reflected in public records and it is important that they are properly maintained.

It is also worth noting that family archives can be repositories that collect records relating to the family, rather than being custodians of the comprehensive archive generated by the family itself over time. An example of this would be the Brontë Parsonage Museum Library, in Haworth, West Yorkshire, which holds the Brontë Society archives with holdings created by and about the Brontë family. Another example, Keats House in London, collects manuscripts and records relating to Keats and his contemporary poets.

Non-profit and non-governmental sector

Many charities and voluntary action organizations maintain in-house archives of their activities, although these tend to be the ones with larger budgets. Smaller charities may have been able to deposit their records with public archives, but those with a broad geographic coverage often find it difficult to find a repository with a corresponding remit.

Archives of faith traditions, such as the established and non-conformist churches, often have extensive archives, managing them in a manner similar to businesses in line with their specific missions. For example, the East London Mosque and London Muslim Centre Archive holds the archives of the mosque and centre dating back to the early 20th century and the Papal Archives at the Vatican Secret Archives in Rome date back more than a thousand years.

The records of international organizations are very important for studying and understanding international co-operation. Many international organizations have records and archives divisions that are increasingly open to access in person and also online. Examples of these include the World Bank, the Council of Europe and the African Union.

Collecting archives

Organizations which actively acquire and manage archives from different provenances in order to build up primary source material on a subject are known as 'collecting' archives and they may or may not also keep the records of their own organization. Here are some examples:

- The UK National Fairground Archive (attached to the University of Sheffield) is a 'unique collection of material covering all aspects of the culture and history of travelling fairs and entertainment from the 1800s to the present day'.
- Newport Historical Society in Rhode Island was founded in 1854 to 'collect and preserve books, manuscripts, and objects pertaining to Newport's history'.
- The Wellcome Library Archives and Manuscripts holds what the website declares to be 'the most important collection of manuscripts and archives on the history of medicine in Britain'.
- The Open Society Archives in Budapest, Hungary, collects the records of the history of the Cold War, the transition to open societies in Central and Eastern Europe and human rights issues and movements.

In practice the delineation between a collecting archive and an institutional archive (one that primarily supports the management of the organization's own records) is not clear-cut. As we know, an archive repository such as a local government archive often holds multiple archives with different provenances. University archives also often actively seek archives of different provenances which support its research goals. Also many libraries, public as well as private, collect archives. A good example of this is local authority libraries in the UK, which often have a local studies section holding archives relating to the geographical area of the authority.

There are also archives which specialize in taking care of archives in special media, such as digital or audiovisual material. Here are two examples:

- The National Film and Sound Archive of Australia is the statutory authority established to develop and preserve 'a national collection of recorded historic and contemporary sound, moving image and artefact works'.
- The UK Data Archive at the University of Essex collects datasets relating to studies and research in the humanities and social science fields.

This kind of collecting archive often provides an invaluable service to archives which have a statutory or geographical remit to take in records but which may not have the resources to deal with the special requirements of the media. Thus, in the UK, regional sound and film archives are used by local government archives as repositories for their audiovisual records in return for access copies for their reading rooms.

The archives and records scene

Given that the earliest forms of writing have been found to date back to the 27th century BC, and there are references to keeping archives in the Bible, it is safe to assume that archives management is one of the oldest professions. Whilst records management would appear to have only been around since the 20th century, many of the components which make it up will have been practised – more or less effectively – for as long as records have been kept. It is a field of activity and expertise which covers a fascinating and diverse range of archival and recordkeeping traditions and practices, around which an infrastructure of international, national, regional and local educational and resource networks have grown up, including:

- the International Council on Archives and its regional branches
- multinational awareness-raising and action consortia working for access to information and information governance
- regional groups focusing on archives requiring particular technical expertise (e.g., audiovisual archives)

- national associations for those working with, owning or using archives
- national professional associations for archivists and records managers
- educational institutions providing education and training for archivists and records managers
- national and international institutions/groups which focus on technical expertise, for example archival preservation or digital records management.

This section provides an introduction to this invaluable, constantly adapting network of resources and lobbying bodies.

The International Council on Archives

The International Council on Archives (ICA) 'is dedicated to the effective management of records and the preservation, care and use of the world's archival heritage through its representation of records and archive professionals across the globe'.[3] It was formed at the UNESCO headquarters on 9 June 1948 (now celebrated as International Archives Day) as an international NGO. It has an ongoing range of products and services to support archivists and records managers around the world in finding solutions to common challenges.

ICA has published several codes and principles which set out the basis of international best practice for archives and records management. These include:

- **The ICA Code of Ethics** (www.ica.org/?lid=5555&bid=225), which aims to 'establish high standards of conduct for the archival profession'. It was formally adopted in September 1996.
- **The Universal Declaration on Archives** (www.ica.org/?lid=13343&bid=1101), initiated by ICA and adopted by UNESCO in 2011, states that the role of the archives is as custodian of cultural heritage and declares that good records management is essential for democracy.
- **The Principles of Access to Archives,**[4] adopted in 2012, assert the moral and legal right of citizens to access archives.

ICA has 13 regional branches, which enable its members to take a more regional approach to professional co-operation and advocacy whilst supporting the overall aims of ICA. Work in the regions has resulted in products which have been applicable worldwide, for example the *PARBICA Recordkeeping for Good Governance Toolkit* (www.ica.org/?lid=4521&bid=139), developed by ICA's Pacific Region.

There are also 12 professional sections, focusing on areas of expertise or concern such as business archives or archival education and training. The sections also work on projects and develop products which can be used around the world, for example the Section for University Archives' *Who's Who in Archives Globally* site (www.library.illinois.edu/ica-suv/BioSite.php).

The ICA expert groups are smaller, more agile groups of professionals who work on specific, topical areas of archives and records management as part of ICA's professional programme. The professional programme itself is developed and managed by the Programme Commission (PCOM). All sections, branches and expert groups report to and are represented on PCOM.

A final ICA body which should be mentioned is the International Fund for Archival Development (FIDA).[5] FIDA has a limited fund to give 'support to archive institutions and archivists with the greatest development needs'. An example of FIDA's work is delivery of workshops on the Good Governance Toolkit in French-speaking Africa.

ICA holds an annual conference for its members except in the years of Olympic Games, when an international congress is held which is open to everyone. The ICA website is full of information, contacts and resources, although access to some of it is restricted to members.

UNESCO Memory of the World Programme

> **Documentary heritage:** 'items which are: moveable . . . ; made up of signs/codes, sounds and/or images; preservable (the carriers are non-living); reproducible and migratable; the product of a deliberate documenting process'.
>
> UNESCO

UNESCO established the Memory of the World (MoW) Programme[6] in 1992 to address threats to the preservation of, and access to, documentary heritage around the world. This was in recognition of the ongoing threats such as deterioration of condition due to age, use and the physical environment (however carefully controlled) but also of the impact of war, civil unrest and natural disaster. The MoW vision is that documentary heritage belongs to all, should be preserved and should be accessible to everyone. Its mission is to facilitate preservation, assist universal access and to increase awareness worldwide of the existence and significance of documentary heritage. The MoW Programme:

- selects items for and maintains the Memory of the World Register
- identifies, fosters partnerships for and manages projects relating to the Programme, for example in the area of using contemporary technology to reproduce (and therefore protect) documentary heritage

- produces guidance and other technical documentation
- oversees the award of the Jikji Prize, which recognizes contribution to the 'preservation and accessibility of documentary heritage as a common heritage of humanity'
- publicizes the work of the Programme with a view to raising awareness of the value of documentary heritage.

There is an International Advisory Committee, which has overall responsibility for planning and implementing the MoW Programme. The Director-General of UNESCO convenes biennial meetings of the 12 members, who serve in a personal capacity and are selected because of their work 'in the field of safeguarding documentary heritage'. There are two sub-committees, the Technical and the Marketing Sub-Committees. There are also national and regional MoW Committees.

The International Memory of the World Register was established in 1995 and accessions are approved by the International Advisory Committee. The *Memory of the World Guidelines* (available on the MoW webpages[7]) explain that rather than a competitive process, each item proposed is assessed against a set of criteria and a country can only nominate two items for each annual call. The criteria provide a useful overview of the characteristics of archives. There are also regional and national Memory of the World registers, established in recognition of the fact that a single international register is too unwieldy to manage and to acknowledge that documentary heritage may be of regional or national significance. These registers are managed by the regional and national MoW Committees.

The Memory of the World Programme offers a range of opportunities to those institutions successful in gaining a place on one of the registers. It gives international recognition to the value of the archives, publicly marks the archive for preservation priorities, ensures that access (either directly or via surrogate) is given and enhances resource leverage. In addition, the MoW Programme website has a number of useful reports and guidelines.

Open Government Partnership

The Open Government Partnership is a multilateral initiative that aims to 'secure concrete commitments from governments to promote transparency, empower citizens, fight corruption, and harness new technologies to strengthen governance'. Launched in 2011 with eight founding members, it now has 66 countries. It has a steering committee made up of governments and civil society organizations. Members have to endorse the Open Government Declaration, which elaborates on the goals cited above, and are obliged to deliver a country action plan for open government which is developed with public consultation and must provide independent reporting on their progress going forward. They also have to make concrete commitments which reflect the four core open government principles of transparency, citizen participation, accountability and technology and innovation.

DLM Forum

The DLM Forum was created in 1994 as a joint initiative by the European Commission and EU member states' national archives. The acronym came from the French 'Données Lisible par Machine' (Machine Readable Data) and at the time DLM's work focused on the challenges of managing electronic records. Since then it has developed into the DLM Foundation, a 'subscription-based community' not only of European national archives but also other public and private bodies interested in archive, records, document and information lifecycle management within and beyond Europe. Its remit has widened to encompass information governance and the acronym now stands for Document Lifecycle Management.

The DLM Forum holds member meetings in the spring and autumn which have a conference format. Once every three years a three-day forum replaces one of these meetings. The meetings are usually hosted by the country holding the EU presidency. MoReq2010®, DLM's flagship product, is a European specification for computerized record systems. DLM certifies systems as complying with the specification via accredited test centres. The DLM website (www.dlmforum.eu) is a useful source of standards and guidance on records and information management.

The International Association of Francophone Archives

L'Association Internationale des Archives Francophones (www.aiaf.org/accueil) or AIAF is an international pressure group for Francophone archives. Its members are both individuals and institutions carrying out or concerned with managing archives and records. One of its major projects is the Francophone archives portal (PIAF), which offers e-learning, training, bibliographic and professional resources. AIAF was formed in 1989 in Madrid at one of the International Council on Archives annual Round Table (CITRA) meetings. Its mission is to promote and develop co-operation between those working with Francophone archives.

Professional associations, centres of expertise and pressure groups

The landscape in which archives and records management operates is constantly changing, depending on government policy, public opinion, funding streams and its position in the wider information management and governance arena. Some countries have independent over-arching 'archive councils' or quasi-public bodies that have responsibility for developing, promoting and funding archive standards and initiatives, possibly together with the other heritage fields such as museums and libraries. Universities or governments may develop expertise in areas such as conservation and preservation of traditional archive formats, digital recordkeeping or disaster prevention and recovery which is accessible to the rest of the archives and records management sector. For those working with archives and records it is important to become familiar with the landscape, regardless of what country they are working in, so as to keep abreast of current developments, practice and standards, to access specialist expertise when needed and to forge alliances and partnerships in managing the holdings. It is impossible to paint this landscape in one seminal, time-defying portrait but this section offers a broad-brush sketch of the types of organizations there are, with some concrete examples.

Professional associations

Technically a professional association is an organization comprising of professionals in the field with a mission and goals that focus on advancing the profession and supporting the professional members. To this end professional associations typically carry out a range of services and activities including, for example:

- requirement of a qualification or qualifications recognized by the profession as being necessary to conduct professional work
- a code of conduct or ethics
- a continuing professional development framework and/or a registration or certification scheme to continuously assess professionals against a competency framework
- award of fellowship status to recognize exceptional service to the profession
- advocacy of the profession and of professional issues to policy-makers
- awareness-raising about the profession and archives and records management with the wider population
- development of professional tools, standards and guidance
- publication of newsletters and professional journals
- organization of conferences (and governance meetings)
- facilitation of special interest groups.

However, this is a very purist definition of a professional association and many professional associations admit institutions as well as individual professionals and allow suppliers and consultants full membership and voting rights.

The Archives and Records Association (ARA, www.archives.org.uk) describes itself as 'the lead professional body for archivists, archive conservators and records managers in the United Kingdom and Ireland'. It was formed out of the 2010 merger of the National Council on Archives, the Association of Chief Archivists in Local Government and the Society of Archivists. It offers a mature example of a professional body with an entry qualification accreditation process, a registration scheme for new professionals, a code of ethics, a competency framework and pilot CPD (continuing professional development) scheme, established special interest groups and regional structures, a well established, peer-reviewed journal, annual conferences and an advocacy programme which includes parliamentary lobbying and an annual archive awareness campaign.

The Information and Records Management Society (www.irms.org.uk) began in 1983 as the Records Management Society. Membership is open to 'all those concerned with records and information, regardless of their professional or organizational status or qualifications . . . organizations wishing to develop records or information systems and those that provide services in these fields'. Its mission focuses on providing leadership to champion and promote records and information management and support professional development. It has regional branches, a bi-monthly *Bulletin*, and has a partnership arrangement with a publisher to produce the *Records Management Journal*. There is also an accreditation scheme to recognize members' professional competencies through peer assessment.

Other Anglophone national professional associations that should be noted are the **Society of American Archivists** (founded in 1936), the **Australian Society of Archivists** and the **Association of Canadian Archivists** (both established in 1975). **ARMA International** (established in 1953) is the predominantly American professional association for records managers, although the 'international' in its title reflects a membership from over 30 other countries. All of these are run along the same lines as the UK professional associations, with similar services and advocacy work. Canada also has the **Association des archivistes du Québec** (founded in 1967). It is a professional organization for French-Canadians, working to support the archives and records management profession and to advocate its cause and work with government and other stakeholders. Other Canadian provinces and territories also have their own professional associations.

Centres of expertise

Many countries have centres of expertise that offer services (possibly at a price) to archives and advice to archivists and records managers. For many years the British Library in the UK funded the **Preservation Advisory Centre**, which offered subsidized training courses in all areas of conservation and archival preservation, as well as publishing a very comprehensive set of guidance on its web pages. Sadly it was forced to close in 2014 due to budget cuts at the British Library. The New Zealand National Library has set up a similar body in its own **National Preservation Office**.

Pressure groups

Although archives and records management professionals are often very active in action groups in the field, there is a set of stakeholders which cannot be described as professional associations. In the UK at least, some of these have existed for many years.

The British Records Association (www.britishrecordsassociation.org.uk) was founded in 1932 and promotes 'the interests of archives and archives users at the national level'; thus its members include not only professional archivists but also librarians and others responsible for managing archives, as well as owners of records and researchers. To this end it provides advice on the care of archives, organizes an annual conference and produces a range of publications, including a journal, *Archives*. The Association's Records Preservation Section advises owners and custodians of archives as to the best place to deposit them and can also help to physically transfer the material.

The Business Archives Council, established in 1934, describes its goals as 'the preservation of business records of historical importance, supplying advice and information on business archives and records, encouraging interest in and study of business history and archives and to provide a forum for the custodians and users of business archives' (www.businessarchivescouncil.org.uk). The Council produces a number of surveys of records of major UK industries, such as banking and brewing, and also publishes a journal, *Business Archives*, every six months. It organizes conferences, seminars and symposiums and training days and workshops. Its members are a combination of archive owners, professional archivists and records managers and researchers.

Archives for London 'brings together everyone interested in archives in or about London – users, practitioners and enthusiasts' (www.archivesforlondon.org). It is an example of a geographically based archives pressure or supporters' group. It offers a series of seminars and visits, as well as an annual conference, and works with other organizations on initiatives and programmes that fall within its remit.

Some countries have pressure groups working for archives and records management at the national level. For example, the **Canadian Council of Archives** (www.cdncouncilarchives.ca) is an independent body made up of representatives from the Canadian provinces and territories, as well as the National Archives, the Association of Canadian Archivists and the Association des archivistes du Québec. It manages various funds to support archives and records management projects.

Records management and archival education and training

The people who look after archives and manage records come from many different educational and cultural backgrounds. Depending on at what level they are working and whether the physical characteristics of the records require specialized expertise, they will have more or less technical, practical and intellectual skills and experience. This book obviously aims at giving beginners and newcomers to archives and records management a good basic introduction, but it cannot cover all of the professional competencies which the discipline encompasses. This section aims to provide an overview of the field and some of the possible routes to further training, knowledge and continuing professional development.

What do we need to know?

In order to manage records and archives we need to have knowledge and skills in the following areas:

- **palaeography:** the skill of being able to read historical handwriting
- **languages:** archaic languages such as Latin or Middle High German, other languages in which the records are written, for example in dual-language countries such as Canada (French and English) or Wales (Welsh and English)
- **computer skills:** these are invaluable in managing records and archives to support the creation and use of finding aids, access, preservation management and control through the lifecycle; more advanced technical skills are required to manage electronic records
- **preservation management:** the physical protection of records and archives in all media and formats, including disaster prevention and recovery, security, handling and use policy and guidelines, environmental and storage standards and cleaning and conservation considerations
- **appraisal:** deciding which records to keep permanently in the archive and when to destroy non-archival records

- **collecting policy:** high-level decisions about what archives to take in
- **acquisition and accessioning:** deposit agreements between record owners and archival custodians; clear documentation on the point of receipt
- **archival processing, arrangement and description:** documenting records and archives in order to manage them and make them accessible to others
- **access provision:** use of archives by researchers, outreach activities to raise awareness about the holdings
- **recordkeeping systems:** understanding how recordkeeping systems work, the relationship between activities and records; creating and maintaining paper and digital filing systems; organizing and managing records effectively; setting destruction deadlines
- **advocacy and marketing:** justification and awareness-raising to ensure archives and records management is resourced, adopted and embedded and archives are funded, protected and used.

Another way of looking at the knowledge and skills needed to manage archives and records is through the development of a competency standard. The Archives and Records Association has recently published a Competency Framework (www.archives.org.uk/careers/cpd.html), which classifies the 36 competencies considered necessary for managing records and archives into ten functions within three areas, as follows:

1 **Organizational**
   (a) governance and planning
   (b) monitoring and evaluation
   (c) personal development
2 **Process**
   (a) processing/managing current or semi-current records in all media and formats
   (b) processing/managing archival records in all media and formats
   (c) preserving records and archives in all media and formats
   (d) conserving archives
3 **User/stakeholder**
   (a) understanding users and stakeholders
   (b) delivering a service to users
   (c) engaging users.

Career paths

A sound education at the point of entry into the profession; competency-based training for continuing professional development and involvement in research-

> based enquiry and knowledge creation all have roles in developing and sustaining well-rounded professionals, to the greater benefit of the profession as a whole.
>
> Karen Anderson, *Education and Training for Records Professionals,* June 2006

There are a number of ways to gain the skills and knowledge to work in the archives and records workforce and/or to become a recognized qualified professional. Looking at the teaching, medical and legal professions, which are more numerous and better-established than ours, the elements in qualifying as a professional include the following:

- theory (education, study)
- practical application (training, practicals)
- probation (the newly educated/trained phase)
- keeping up with new developments, techniques and practice
- membership of an advocacy body for the profession
- voluntary or compulsory 'policing' by a regulating body to an agreed or accepted standard.

All of these elements should be in place for recognized qualified professionals, but many of them are accessible and desirable for anyone working with records and archives.

Training

> **Training:** the acquisition of knowledge and skills that enables learners to carry out their work; tends to focus on job skills and awareness-raising.

Training in looking after archives and records management takes a variety of forms and can be delivered by a range of providers (for example the professional associations described above). It is usually of a practical nature and has a small, focused learning remit aiming to teach participants specific competencies to be able to operate effectively in one operational area. An example might be training in disaster prevention and recovery. Training might also be a more general introduction or overview, such as the Basic Archive Skills Training Day offered by the Archive-Skills Consultancy.[8] Training is useful for both qualified and recognized professionals and para-professionals. Providers of archives and records management training include the professional associations, universities and consultants.

Tertiary education

> **Education:** following systematic instruction or intellectual and moral training designed to give a broad and/or deep understanding of the topics covered. Usually associated with children and young people.

In the UK, as in many other parts of the world, it is possible to study archives and records management in universities. This tends to be at postgraduate level and students gain a postgraduate diploma or, increasingly, a master's degree in archives and/or records management. In other parts of the world, it might be an undergraduate degree, but the model is to have a range of universities offering students a choice of not only where to study but also of the content of the study. In the UK the Archives and Records Association (ARA) has an accreditation framework for the university courses and students are well advised to study on one of the accredited programmes. This also happens in Australia, where the Australian Society of Archivists[9] accredits courses.

Another model for tertiary education is that of a dedicated archives school. In France many archivists are educated at the École Nationale des Chartes,[10] founded in 1821, part of the Sorbonne, offering a three-year master's degree. As a public institution under a ministerial charter from the Department of Higher Education and Research it is very prestigious and on acceptance its students are enrolled into the French civil service for ten years. In Germany there is the Archivschule in Marburg (http://archivschule.de), founded in 1949. It is a Hessen state institution operating as a technical university awarding students from the German civil service a bachelor's or master's degree, depending on their grade.

In the UK it is very hard to be recognized as a professional archivist without an academic qualification from one of the ARA-accredited university courses, particularly if you started your career in recent decades.

Professional recognition

Another way of attaining professional status is by a rigorous accreditation or certification process. The UK Information and Records Management Society has an accreditation scheme which offers 'professional recognition to any individual member working in the fields of records management, . . . any other allied profession' by providing evidence of their competence and experience. Successful candidates are entitled to the post-nominal AMIRMS (Accredited Member of the Information and Records Management Society).

In the USA, the Academy of Certified Archivists (ACA, see www.certifiedarchivists.org), originally set up by the Society of American Archivists but now an independent body, describes itself as the 'certifying organization of professional archivists'. Certification involves providing evidence of appropriate tertiary education (not necessarily in archives and records management) and experience (which is longer if candidates' education has not been in the field) as well as sitting a three-hour exam consisting of 100 multiple-choice questions.

Similarly, the Institute of Certified Records Managers (ICRM, see www.icrm.org), 'an international certifying organization of and for professional records and information managers' runs a scheme for professional recognition of its members. The ICRM was originally an ARMA International body which is now fully independent. Applicants for ICRM certification must have a bachelor's degree or a substantial amount of relevant experience and demonstrate a range of work experience falling into four or more specified categories. Suitably qualified applicants must then pass a six-part examination. Both of these examples require re-certification at regular intervals and thus operate as continuing professional development (CPD) schemes as well.

Continuing professional development

CPD is a regime of training, research and contribution to the individual's own professional arena which aims to update, expand and enhance skills, knowledge and expertise. The goals are to ensure currency of knowledge and skills and competency, to be able to perform more difficult roles, sometimes to move into a new role or job altogether and to give confidence in the profession as a whole.

CPD can be pursued as part of an organized scheme. One example is the CILIP (Chartered Institute of Library and Information Professionals) revalidation scheme[11] for its Chartered Members. Another example is Records and Information Professionals Australasia (RIMPA) which has a compulsory CPD scheme for all its members, because the organization believes 'it is vital that Professional Members remain current in the dynamic field of records management. This goes beyond initial qualification and implies a system of Continuing Professional Development'.[12] The scheme involves members providing evidence of CPD over a three-year cycle. On successful completion of CPD requirements, members receive a professional membership certificate which is valid for three years.

In practice most people in the archives and records management workforce are pursuing CPD, even if it is not part of a recognized scheme. Professional development opportunities include training courses, active membership of the professional organizations, reading the professional literature and doing something new in the workplace for the first time.

Working with records and archives

We live in the information age. Modern technology allows us to create and have access to a wealth of information, including records and archives, in many different media and formats with very little hindrance. This could be digitally via the internet and mobile technology or in person via libraries, archives and even directly in the offices of creators under information rights legislation such as Freedom of Information or Data Protection. Technology also allows the information to be duplicated and manipulated such that the sheer quantity of information (and therefore records and archives) has become a real challenge to manage not only on an organizational level but also for individuals and communities or society as a whole.

This book is concerned with how we manage records effectively to ensure they are fit for purpose, are available when needed, can be relied upon in everyday business and are kept only as long as required to support business, work or the process, unless they are of archival value. It is also concerned with how we manage and protect those records that have been selected for the archives so as to ensure that they remain accessible to employees, business managers and owners, the public and generations of unknown users to come.

It goes without saying that if we decide to keep records permanently as archives because of their value in providing key evidence of the history of the creating body, we need to look after them very carefully. Moreover, it is likely that archives will have many different people looking after them over time because we anticipate them outlasting the lifespan of a single human being. Good archival management is documented and transparent to allow different custodians to care for the archives in a consistent way over time.

Challenges and issues

The information age holds many challenges and issues for those of us who care about looking after and/or using records and archives. Table 1.2 shows the kinds of questions that concern creators, users and managers of records and archives – and which this book aims to address.

There are many aspects to recordkeeping and archives management and the main concerns are outlined here. They will be covered in more detail later in the book.

Space

We need to ensure that there is physical room and/or server/offline storage for current and non-current records and archives. We also need to know that it is appropriate, secure space and it is efficient and cost-effective.

Table 1.2 *Challenges and issues in managing archives and records*

	Creator	***Manager***	***User***
Records	• what to create? • how to create, what to include? • what format or medium? • how to keep, file, classify? • who to share with? • enough space? • enough budget? • reliable records? • how long to keep records? • is it legal to keep records? • is it legal to destroy records? • can information be found?	• enough space? • enough budget? • reliable records? • how long to keep records? • is it legal to keep records? • is it legal to destroy records? • whether to scan records? • can information be found? • sensitive records? • access to records	• what records are there? • where are records? • what format or medium? • who created records? • reliable records? • usable, accessible records? • OK to copy?
Archives	• which are archives? • need to keep archives? • how to keep archives? • need to share archives? • how to share archives? • how valuable are the archives?	• need to keep archives? • where to keep archives? • catalogues, indexes, finding aids • allow access to archives? • access rights management • advertising archives • protecting archives	• what archives are there? • where are archives? • what format or medium? • who created archives? • reliable archives? • usable, accessible archives? • OK to copy?

Creation

It is very important that records are created as necessary and appropriate to support human activity (be it commercial, social or private) and that they document what is needed for the activity to happen or continue to happen, as well as provide reliable evidence of what occurred. It is also important that records and archives are created well. First of all, we need to know where the information came from and its reliability and secondly, the medium and format need to be appropriate for the use the record will be put to, as well as robust enough to survive for as long as needed. Records – and archives – must have a few pieces of crucial descriptive information, including things such as the creator and the date. This kind of information is called metadata and it may be contained within the record, or associated with it via a finding aid such as an index or a computer system or program.

Access

Current records are usually primarily of interest to a select group or groups of people, regardless of whether the records are archival or not. Organizations and record creators and users save or file records in systems where they can be accessed by everyone who needs to see them – or for access to be controlled and limited as necessary. Archives, particularly the archives of public bodies, are usually freely available to anyone. It is advisable to manage access carefully, both to ensure the safety of the archives and to gain a body of knowledge about use trends and levels. Private archives are not necessarily open to everyone to consult. Finding aids, such as indexes or file lists and metadata, can be used to facilitate and control access to records and archives, regardless of their age or status. Another aspect of access is promotion of the archive holdings to attract new audiences into the reading room and to use any online services.

Content management

We have already mentioned the role of metadata and finding aids in facilitating access to records and archives. In general, it is more efficient if users know what sort of information is in the records or archives before they begin looking at them. It also protects the archives against unnecessary wear and tear caused by the need to check whether the records are of interest or not. One way of facilitating the process is through accurate and meaningful file or document/folder titles. The other way is through metadata and finding aids such as classification schemes and indexes. A good, well thought out and maintained, recordkeeping system will be easy to use. Creators will know where to file or save records and users will be able to retrieve records accurately and easily. Archives which come from good recordkeeping systems may well have original finding aids but if there are no contemporary finding aids, we need to create some in order to make the content accessible.

Legal situation

There are many legal issues associated with archives and records. We need to think about ownership and physical custody, as well as intellectual property rights. By law, certain types of records must be created and kept, whilst some records must be kept securely and/or destroyed if certain conditions are not met. Whilst those of us managing records and looking after archives cannot be expected to provide legal advice, we need to be aware of the relevant legal obligations.

Maintenance

Records and archives need ongoing management. Recordkeeping systems such as physical file stores and digital drives can become disorganized and unreliable if they are not consistently added to according to the method of organization. The same is true for archives, but for archives there is also a higher risk of physical deterioration. With digital records, the speed of technological advance is such that we need to ensure that even very recently created records can continue to be accessed and read over time.

Records management

> **Records management:** a comprehensive regime which controls records through their lifecycle, including: deciding what records to create; organizing them so that they support business needs and authorized retrieval; evaluating and imposing retention requirements; documented destruction or designation as archives.

Records management is concerned with having effective control over records to ensure that they are created to provide reliable evidence as needed, can be exploited as an information resource, are kept in accordance with any applicable legislation and are destroyed when no longer needed – unless deemed archival. It is a discipline which is applied in a real-life environment, working with individuals and groups whose priorities are not necessarily having a tidy filing system. It requires a certain knowledge and experience as well as a particular set of skills but it is not an arcane or esoteric science. It's a very practical function.

Records management can be broken down into a set of activities, all of which are needed to achieve that control over the records. The main building blocks are outlined below.

Needs analysis

A needs analysis can be used to justify records management where there is no existing formal provision. It involves a study of the functions, records and recordkeeping habits and culture of the organization with a view to identifying areas of risk and inefficiency and to put into place measures for improvement.

Records survey

The records survey is a systematic information-gathering process which focuses on what record users and creators do, what records they create and use to support their work and how they organize and keep them. The survey provides the basis for developing the records management system.

Appraisal

Records need to be appraised to establish access rights, sharing requirements and how long they should be retained. This process leads to the development of the tools, such as lists of retention periods, together with the procedures necessary to establish and inform consistent and appropriate record access and security management across the organization.

Current recordkeeping systems

Records really need to be captured and controlled from the moment they are created. The way we do this is in good physical filing systems or well organized computer systems. There is no inherent right way or wrong way to organize records – the system will depend on the nature of the work or activity being recorded and supported as well as the abilities and habits of the creator(s) or culture of the organization. The important thing is to be consistent, keep up with the filing and to document the system so that anyone can easily use it.

Non-current recordkeeping systems

Non-current records are the records that are no longer needed to support the work. On the other hand, they may need to be retained for legal reasons, or for infrequent access to answer queries or review the history of activity. Non-current records are closed: that is to say, they are no longer added to because the case, project or work cycle is over. The trick is to make sure that non-current records are identified and listed in finding aids that ensure that any given record can be easily retrieved if required.

Storage

Records management involves selecting and managing appropriate record storage, be it physical, onsite, off-site or even outsourced, or digital in the form of servers, drives, tape libraries or residing in the cloud. Whilst non current records that are ultimately due for destruction do not require the very high standard physical environment that archival records need, they still need an environment that is secure from unauthorized access and ensures that they are accessible and readable for as long as they are needed. Different media require different storage environments.

Disposal

Disposal can mean destruction or removal to archives. Records which are not of archival value should be destroyed when they no longer serve a useful operational purpose and do not need to be kept for legal or contractual reasons. This must be done in such a way that they cannot be accessed again and there are no copies left. This process must also be clearly documented with authorization and destruction details. If this final process is not well managed and documented, it undermines the whole recordkeeping effort. Obviously if records are archival, they will be processed and documented according to archives management procedures.

Vital records and emergency planning

Records management plays a crucial role in emergency planning, because it allows the identification of those records vital to business continuity and the development of a strategy to protect them. It also feeds into disaster prevention planning and strategies for dealing quickly and effectively with the adverse results of any disaster threatening the safety and longevity of archival, business-critical and other vital records.

Awareness-raising

One of the most important aspects of records management is persuading stakeholders of the need to manage records. We need to be able to justify records management throughout the organization.

Ongoing review

Organizations are continually changing and developing, and the records which support business functions and activities will evolve at the same rate. Therefore records management systems need to be regularly reviewed to ensure that they remain fit for purpose, cover all organizational records and make the best use of recordkeeping solutions.

Looking after archives

Managing archives effectively, to ensure that they are both accessible and protected against the wear and tear of use and the natural deterioration due to age that impacts all matter, requires a range of skills and expertise which can be categorized into a number of functional areas.

Preservation management

This function is perhaps the most important aspect of managing archives, since we aim to keep them forever, so we need to take measures to ensure their survival. It involves preventing deterioration or disintegration, providing an environment that protects the records physically and ensures their longevity, disaster prevention and recovery, use policy and guidelines, good handling practices, conservation considerations and a holistic collections care strategy.

Appraisal

Deciding which records to keep permanently in the archive is a fundamental aspect of their management, since it involves judgement about the value of the records and an appreciation of legal, business, cultural and societal considerations, combined with a knowledge of archival appraisal principles. We select those few of all the creator's records that represent and provide evidence of the 'story'.

Collecting policy

We need to decide what kind of archives we want to keep in order to match the organization's and archive repository's aims to resources. This involves describing the scope of the archives holdings, both currently and as it is envisioned in the future.

Acquisition

We need to ensure that we have clear acquisition agreements when we take in new archives so that ownership and/or custody is legal and we know how the records may be used. The agreement must include physical and intellectual property rights.

Accessioning

This is about initial documentation or registration of archives, which acts as a basic control or accession record giving details of creator, quantity, content and location, the basic contextual and authentication information needed for coherent, robust and global collection management.

Archival processing, arrangement and description

This is a large and often challenging competency area which involves gathering information about records and archives in order to manage them and make them accessible to others. It is a slow, painstaking task which results in a range of finding aids and control documentation. It requires research and analysis of the records to understand their interrelationships and the way the creator produced and used them in order to derive information about the content and context of the records. The resulting archival finding aids should act as maps for researchers and users so that they can locate records of interest to them.

Access provision

We keep archives so that people can consult and use them. Providing access involves helping people use the archives, providing the environment and supplementary resources for users, complying with legal and societal obligations and protecting the archives when being used. It is also about more active outreach activities to raise awareness about holdings, to ensure that they are known about and used as much as possible. It requires good finding aids or recordkeeping systems, an understanding of the content of the individual components of the holdings and of the ways people might wish to consult and use the material, as well as having a vision of the ways in which the records might be used. Moreover, it involves an understanding of intellectual property rights and conditions as well as the more subtle issues around privacy and confidentiality.

Advocacy

This is a crucial part of archives management. It involves ensuring that we have the resources to look after the archives, gaining and retaining support to maintain the archives and mobilizing politicians, managers and citizens as champions of the archives.

Record creators and archive users

There can be a symbiotic dependency between creators and records managers, as well as between archivists and researchers, but the two can also seem to have conflicting goals. It is useful to consider where the creators of the records are coming from and what archives users expect, because it helps us to manage records and archives more effectively.

Record creators

We have already considered the concerns of record creators, identifying issues such as what records to create, how and where to keep them for how long and finding them when needed. Most creators have a very pragmatic approach to recordkeeping and do the minimum necessary to file them, their main concern being the ability to retrieve them. Because they create the records, and because they use the recordkeeping system regularly – if they haven't created it as well – the knowledge of how to use the system and retrieve records often exists only in their heads. When the system is shared with so many people that a group discipline is needed, or when the only person who knows how it works is inaccessible, the risk of not documenting the system becomes apparent.

Understanding the reasons why records are created and organized helps us to develop more effective recordkeeping systems which are also easier to use.

There are a number of factors or questions to consider in trying to understand the organization's record creation and management habits. The organization, what it does and its culture influence its recordkeeping profoundly. Understanding whether the organization is governmental, international, non-governmental, business or charity is relatively easy but understanding the individual corporate culture of an organization is more challenging. Once we understand the organization, its mission, priorities and way of working, we can see cause and effect on records creation and management – and begin to make positive changes as needed. Table 1.3 gives some basic questions and possible answers to help understand how and why organizations create and manage records the way they do.

Archive users

Archive users cannot be easily characterized and their research interests are myriad. However, we don't need a detailed understanding of the various subgroups because, whilst we want to help them use the archives, we also want the archives to be an independent testimony to the history of the organization or individual. We also want our custody and care to be as objective and neutral as possible to ensure that the integrity and independence remain for generation upon generation of users, whose research interests and methods we cannot possibly guess.

Archive users are generally not interested in the whole archive or all the holdings in a repository. They are interested in subjects, names or places, not interested in how the various parts of the archive relate to each other or the fact that all the items in an archive have the same provenance. They often don't understand why some of the records they imagine should have been either created or kept do not actually exist.

In order to provide access, we generally develop two layers of finding aids. One is a map or schema of how the records are related to each other, usually based on organizational functions or the separate activities of the family or

Table 1.3 *How organizations create and manage records*

	Government	Business	Private Individual/family
Which records are created?	• legislation • policy • agreements and frameworks with citizens, industry, foreign countries • routine correspondence, receipts, forms, licences • council and committee minutes • regulations, inspection and revenue-raising records • health and education records	• governing board records • production, operational or service records • administrative support records	• key 'life' records (birth, naturalization, marriage, death, passport, National Health Service card) • records of qualifications and achievements • personal correspondence, diaries • home administration records • work and/or social life records
Who is creating records?	• employees • citizens • contractors	• staff • customers	• individuals and family • friends • employers and authorities
How are they being organized?	• computers and paper filing cabinets • Electronic Records Management System (ERMS) • in old registry systems • all doing own thing • following standards	• on computer may have ERMS • in paper systems • systemized • disorganized • following standards	• on computer • in paper systems • systemized • disorganized
Who are the records shared with?	• security classified • colleagues in department or within authority • colleagues across government • public	• colleagues • customers • contractors • associated businesses • commercially sensitive	• family • friends • organizations to/which they belong/interact • authorities
What recordkeeping resources are there?	• usually one or two posts • some IT support • may have ERMS	• records manager with team • ad hoc consultant support	• time of individuals
How long are the records kept?	• according to retention schedule based on various laws and guidance • archive facilities and expertise	• according to retention schedule based on various laws and guidance • financial records according to regulation	• ad hoc solution to keep volume manageable
What are the legal issues?	• Freedom of Information law • environmental regulations • public records Acts • health and safety law • financial Acts and regulation • data protection	• health and safety law • financial Acts and regulation • sector-specific legislation • data protection	• proof not breaking law and meeting legal obligations • proof of rights

individual. This helps us to preserve the evidence and knowledge of how the records arose from the creator's activity. The second layer is a detailed description of the content, which may be indexed manually or, increasingly, part of a computerized system with a range of search functions.

Meeting expectations that records should have been created when they were not is almost impossible. Explaining why records that once existed are no longer around can easily be demonstrated if the right archives and records management policies are in place.

Having said it is not necessary – or even possible – to choose the archives we keep because of the research interests of our users, it is useful to think about the main categories of research that users come to archives to pursue, since this can help to meet their needs. Table 1.4 gives the main categories of archive users, suggesting their motivation and characteristics.

Table 1.4 *Archive users and their perspectives*

User/Researcher group	Perspectives
Academics	• usually highly educated, organized, focused • may be experienced archive users • often expect archives to contain material relevant to their research and be organized as they want
Genealogists	• could have any level of education, organizational skills and experience of archives • may be easily satisfied if lots of personal name indexes – or disappointed if not • new genealogists need coaching
Journalists, film and TV producers	• confident and empowered • expect records of subjects interested in to be there and organized in ways they imagine • don't distinguish between archives, books and artefacts • may expect special treatment without offering remuneration for services received • can be experienced researchers
Schoolchildren	• should come with teacher or parent • don't know (or need to know) complexities of archival description • probably need resources based on school curriculum • offers opportunity to introduce them positively to archives
Students	• could be highly educated, organized, focused, depending on level and reason doing research • can be inexperienced or more experienced • may be interested in course-related materials • may need lots of help if beginning research
Freedom of Information/Open Data/Big Data researchers	• ordinary citizens • very varied in terms of education and experience of using archives • focused on particular information in archives/records not records in context • may need to think laterally to find what they are looking for
Personal history researchers (e.g. for adoption details)	• probably inexperienced in archive use • probably anxious or stressed • interested in names, institutional records • need sensitive and/or appropriately qualified support
Local historians	• can be very knowledgeable and know archives better than archivists • may have own collections of archive materials • may expect archives to be organized like a local studies library
House history	• very focused on own house • probably not experienced in using archives • may be frustrated at lack of archival resources

Round-up

We have now explored the concepts behind managing archives and records, looked at the wider context of this field of activity, examined its constituent parts (albeit in summary) and considered the creators' and users' points of view. It is time to look at the principles and activities required to create and organize current records, control and manage non-current records and look after archives over time.

Notes

1 http://discovery.nationalarchives.gov.uk/find-an-archive.
2 www.nationalarchives.gov.uk/archives-sector/accreditation.htm.
3 www.ica.org.
4 www.ica.org/13619/toolkits-guides-manuals-and-guidelines/principles-of-access-to-archives.html.
5 www.ica.org/12586/fida-funding-and-support/fida-funding-and-support.html.
6 www.unesco.org/new/en/communication-and-information/flagship-project-activities/memory-of-the-world/homepage.
7 http://unesdoc.unesco.org/images/0012/001256/125637e.pdf.
8 www.archive-skills.com/training/index.php.
9 https://www.archivists.org.au/learning-publications/accredited-courses and https://www.archivists.org.au/documents/item/203.
10 www.enc-sorbonne.fr/fr/rubrique-ecole/ecole-nationale-chartes.
11 www.cilip.org.uk/cilip/jobs-careers/professional-registration/levels-professional-registration/revalidation.
12 http://rimpa.com.au/professional-development/cpd-scheme.

CHAPTER 2
Managing current records

Introduction

Current records: records which are being used to support current business and organizational needs. Also known as active records.

This chapter is about recordkeeping from the perspective of the people who create and use the records to support their business, personal or social activity. It is quite difficult to draw an absolute line between the recordkeeping activities for current records and those for non-current records, but for the purposes of this book, they are distinguished not only according to their currency but also by the owners. We will look at good systems, how we can establish or improve them and how they should be maintained and reviewed. With the advent of computers, information and records manifest not only in physical formats (for example paper or magnetic tape) but also in digital format. Therefore we will address managing current records in this challenging hybrid environment. The section also covers security issues and introduces vital records management as far as it is necessary as part of current recordkeeping.

In contemporary organizations records, especially digital records, are created at an incredible rate. They can be used, deleted and misplaced without any organizational control. Much of what end-users think of as records are in fact non-record information, ephemeral records or drafts. Amongst other possibilities, records can be created in the computer system, received in paper copy from outside the organization, formally drawn up on paper or be the result of hand-written amendments to paper print-outs. Thus they may physically reside in disparate locations as well as be rendered in different media. With the rise of computers good administrative staff with filing skills have disappeared. End-users are usually expected to set up and use their own systems, either individually or as teams, and there is rarely any training or guidance unless records management is in place.

Computers have been revolutionary in their impact on the way we conduct business, in terms of automating drudgery, speeding up operations, analysis and improving consistency. However, as the computer systems designers develop more user-friendly applications, any centralized control over record creation and registration becomes increasingly difficult. End-users have, and will continue to have, enormous power over the fate of the records they create and receive – the challenge for archivists and records managers is to convince organizations and individuals of the benefits of sound recordkeeping practice.

Whilst many end-users are excellent recordkeepers, it is the records manager's responsibility to ensure current records management is effective, fit for purpose and integrated into workflows consistently across the organization as a whole, as seamlessly as possible.

In managing current records the records manager is helping end-users to set up and manage:

- the system(s) in which the records are created and maintained
- the organization, identification and naming of the records in the system and the links between them
- the processes and procedures for creating, filing and using the records – and for keeping them safe.

At the same time this needs to be done in a way that is consistent with the organizational culture and any relevant regulations or legislation.

The issue of deciding – and managing – how long records should be kept is handled in Chapter 3, because organizations generally rely on recordkeeping professionals for guidance and to do the work of establishing retention schedules.

Creation

Most people create records in the course of their work and those who don't will create or at least receive a few records in their private lives. Creation is the act of documenting events, activities and decisions. In the paper world it involved writing by hand, or typing, and possibly validating it in some way – for example, with a seal or a signature. In the digital era creation happens when documents are saved onto the system, hard drive or mobile device. Validation is possible, but electronic signatures are generally only used for a very few records where this form of guarantee is important. Table 2.1 gives a few examples of record-creating acts, together with a suggestion of what the resulting record would look like and where it might be located.

We will look at filing practices for both paper and electronic records later, but first, let's look more closely at what 'good' records are and how to ensure that end-users create them. The theory, particularly around digital records, stresses the importance of a number of characteristics that must be present in records. However, when these characteristics are defined and broken down,

Table 2.1 *Acts of record creation*

Act	Record(s)	Medium	Location(s)
Filling out and signing a cheque	• cheque • cheque stub	Paper	• account-holder – payee – payee's bank – account-holder's bank • account-holder's cheque book
Registering online to participate in a training course	• system-generated e-mail to trainer	Digital	• trainer's e-mail system • participant's sent mail
Writing and signing a letter to policy-holder confirming insurance contract	• digital draft • paper signed original • paper copy of signed original	Paper and digital	• company's computer system • company's policy-holder's file • policy-holder's own records

it becomes clear that they are exceedingly difficult to find in many informational objects that we regard as records. Before we look at more practical aspects of record creation, let's look at a list of 'classic' characteristics:

- **purposeful:** the record has been created for a reason and is a necessary part of an activity or function
- **context:** there is a clear relationship between the record, the activity/function, the creator and related activities and records
- **content:** the record documents an event or activity
- **completeness:** the record contains everything necessary to document the activity or decision together with the associated metadata
- **usability:** the record can be accessed without changing, or losing, any of its characteristics
- **authenticity:** the author of the record, and their authority and reason for creating the record, are clear (this characteristic is closely related to reliability and to the principle of provenance)
- **reliability:** the record must be trustworthy, in terms of knowing the creator and context of creation, the accuracy of its content as testimony of the event or activity and its authenticity
- **immutability:** the record cannot be altered once it is created or declared
- **integrity:** the record is complete, authentic and all components are present, in the correct order.

Many of these characteristics, particularly for digital records, require reli information which is held externally to the record itself. As we saw in the section, metadata plays a crucial role in managing records at all stages ir lifecycle:

Metadata: Descriptive information about records and archives. Traditionally this was to be found explicitly in the records (e.g., dates of creation, author, file title) or in related finding aids such as file classification schemes, indexes or archive catalogues. In the digital era, technology is capable of automatically associating metadata with documents, folders and applications within live systems.

In practical terms, defining record characteristics in this way is most useful when working with IT professionals to specify or design a system that will create and manage records. However, even from the brief explanation given for each characteristic in the list above, we can see that they overlap and are co-dependent. The characteristics are also hard to translate into concrete conditions. How, for example, can we ensure the authenticity of a record? Paper records can be signed, sealed or notarized, but digital signature functionality for record-creating systems is not yet widespread.

It is important to remember that most records do not need such stringent validation as signatures and seals. In practice most recordkeeping systems are perfectly reliable and trustworthy because in general terms the creators and users recognize and trust other features of the system necessary for them to use it, for example:

- the author or creator, their role, department and organization or place in the family
- the look and feel of the records – this includes the way they are set out, letter headings, fonts, signatures, logos, etc.
- less apparent metadata, such as the header information attached to e-mail, the document and folder properties
- any file referencing system.

If creators and users are relying on the records in the normal course of business, this lends authenticity and integrity to the records.

Thus, records creation is about ensuring that records are created consistently with a range of characteristics that make them usable and reliable. They should be created in a system, format or medium that will last for as long as the record is needed. The content of the record is important and forms or templates can be used to ensure complete and accurate records. Records are rarely created in a vacuum and therefore there is a need to link them to related records at the time of, or soon after, creation. If more serious validation or authentication is required the use of manual signatures or seals should be weighed against digital validation options. Paper is bulky and the process may be cumbersome, whilst digital signatures and encryption technology may be expensive and hard to introduce.

Current records management is, however, not only dependent on the medium, systems and characteristics of the records being created, but also on the filing and computer systems to which they are attached and in which they are kept.

Filing, classification and file naming

There are three main components of a filing system:

1 the type of records, how they relate to each other and how they are filed (filing rules)
2 how files relate to each other (classification schemes)
3 labels for files and file categories (naming conventions).

> **Filing system:** physical containers or software and intellectual framework together with policy and procedures for organizing and controlling records and groups of records.

Managing current records depends on having a system that is simple, intuitive and reflects the work that the records arise from and support. The system has a physical component – the storage space and the file containers, or the server space – and an 'intellectual' component – the way the records are organized within the system. The storage system itself might be a set of filing cabinets, shelves with box files, an individual's home drive, a team-shared drive, an electronic records management system, a Sharepoint or cloud solution.

> **Intellectual control:** knowing the content of the records and therefore being able to access and manage them. This is achieved through finding aids such as indexes and catalogues, but also through file classification schemes.

Whether physical or digital, the records need to be captured in the system in a structured and systematic way. In the case of current records, this is usually a classification scheme which links records arising from the same function or activity. There may also be a need for more detailed file lists. There should also be some rules around what files are called – because not everyone will use the same term for the same case. For example, if the files are for individuals, will they be named 'surname, first name', according to a running ID number system or by social security or national insurance number? The names given to digital records are particularly important – both for documents as well as folders. This is because it is not possible to browse through digital records in the same way you can flick through a filing cabinet drawer or paper file to find what you are interested in.

Although there are different ways of organizing records, mostly they are grouped together into files because (particularly with paper records) keeping track of each individual record is neither necessary nor cost-effective. It is also efficient to have all the records relating to one case or subject conveniently in one unit. Thus filing systems – which are represented by properly organized folder structures in the digital arena – have become the most common way of controlling large numbers of records.

Setting up or improving filing systems

Let's start with looking at how to set up or improve a filing system.

Reviewing the current situation

An ongoing principle with records and archives management is that it is not possible unless and until you know the size and nature of the material. Therefore the first thing to do when setting up a new system, or trying to improve a system that is not working well, is to review the records and find out what work brings the records about. Looking at the records is a straightforward task, but you will also need to gather information from people creating and using the paper and digital systems.

It is important to include all records in the review, but it can be difficult to identify all the places where records might be kept. In particular, the review needs to look at paper and digital records and the relationships between them in order to identify the master and to establish recommendations aimed at eliminating duplication whilst ensuring the full record is maintained.

Good questions to ask are given in Checklist 2.1:

Checklist 2.1 Setting up or improving filing systems

- Are there record creation and saving procedures?
- Is it easy to tell where to file/save records?
- Is it easy to find records/files?
- Are all records that 'tell the complete story' filed/saved together or at least cross-referenced?
- Are files and sections of the filing system/folder structure complete?
- Are there parallel or duplicate files/folders?
- Is it clear when to open a new file/folder/section, how to do it, who may do it and how it is documented?
- Is there a classification scheme or file plan?
- Does the filing system/folder organization and structure reflect the work of

the department/team?
- Do you need to divide sections of the filing/folder hierarchy?
- Do you need to combine sections or systems?
- What are the main categories of files that need to be included in the system based on the functions and activities of the team? Are they properly represented in the classification scheme or are people having to work around it?

The answers to these questions, together with analysis of the options for organizing the records intellectually and their physical storage locations, form the basis for deciding the best kind of filing system.

Decide on the classification scheme

Classification scheme: list of file categories and sub-categories, based on the nature of the work documented and supported by records and record groupings (files). Also known as the file plan.

Once you know about the records and the work of those creating and using them, you should be in a position to draft or amend the classification scheme (more information on developing different kinds of classification schemes is given later in this chapter). Make sure that the paper and digital systems are mapped to each other and cross-referenced. The scheme should be formally and separately documented and will form part of the filing and records management procedures. The argument that the folder structure on the drive, or the filing cabinet drawer labels, provide all the documentation needed should be resisted – proper documentation is necessary to train and remind users and helps to ensure that everyone using the system takes it seriously. Once you have decided on the classification scheme, you can make the necessary changes.

Organizing or reorganizing the files or folders

If you are setting up a new system from scratch beware of opening files and categories which do not yet have any documentation: begin with the records that are waiting to be filed. If you are essentially deconstructing an existing group of records because the organization doesn't work, you can work through them systematically and re-file them according to the new system. This works for both paper and digital records, but slightly better in the digital arena because it's easier to find space for the skeleton of the new system.

If you are renovating an existing system the tasks will include developing a section of the classification scheme, closing files and opening new ones, and splitting or merging files. Duplicates and old versions can be identified and destroyed. Digital documents can also be given better names.

The process of reorganizing the files can be time-consuming and may also be disruptive to ongoing work and so it should be done quickly but accurately. There also needs to be a plan for filing and retrieval during this reorganization work.

Documentation

When you have implemented the new or improved system, you need to make sure that the documentation is complete. In addition to the classification scheme there will be filing guidelines and naming conventions. Ensure that all staff using the system know how to use it to both file and retrieve records – and that they know where the file plan and other filing procedures can be found. Documentation and training is covered below.

Filing

Filing is about placing individual records in a certain order (for example chronological) inside a file cover, together with other records that also relate to the same business, case or project. Requiring knowledge of the system and the work as well as accuracy and attention to detail, it is crucial for finding records again later.

The practice of filing is probably one of the most underestimated and undervalued activities in modern organizations. It is usually considered to refer to paper records, which are (or should be) systematically placed on files that are classified or organized according to the work of the creating department. Filing is often given to the most junior person in the office, and not infrequently given to temporary staff, neither of whom are best placed to understand the work or the filing system. If there is no one dedicated to doing the filing, then many people will be adding to and consulting files, risking misfiling and missing records. The systems themselves should reflect the work of the department or team and as that work changes the system needs to be adapted with it. These issues are common across both paper and digital filing systems and the problem is exacerbated by duplication within and across the media. Figure 2.1 gives some historical background for filing.

A practical example

In the 21st century the link between digital records and paper records is complicated and difficult to unpick. Unless we examine the links and take steps to eliminate duplication both within and across the media, we will never achieve truly efficient filing systems. If we consider all of the places where

Recordkeeping is not a modern invention: tally sticks have been found dating back to Palaeolithic times; the Shang Dynasty (17th to 11th century BC) maintained records; by the 19th century registry systems were common for governments and large institutions around the world. Registry systems were centralized filing services, either serving the whole organization or operating within departments. Typically there would be a team of trained staff to carry out a range of filing and indexing activities, including:

- opening the mail
- assigning mail to the appropriate file
- forwarding mail to the relevant staff
- receiving and filing copies of outgoing mail
- receiving and filing documents and records
- indexing records
- closing old files
- opening new files
- producing (lending) files to staff.

With the advent of computer technology the efficiency of traditional registries was called into question – what need was there for filing and indexing when computerized systems could search on full text, and when many staff could share and access the same files from their desks?

With the experience of managing electronic records, it is now clear that while the activities and processes carried out in traditional registries needed reinventing for the digital environment, the skills of organizing and tagging records are still needed to ensure records are together with related records and can be found when needed.

Figure 2.1 *The history of filing*

the documentation on a single event, decision or issue might reside, we can easily identify:

- sender's e-mail
- sender's shared drive
- sender's paper filing system
- recipient's e-mail
- recipient's shared drive
- recipient's filing system.

Taking the example of a customer policy manager (CPM) in an insurance company who has sold a policy and needs to get the policy signed by the customer, let's focus on this documentation and map the process behind it. For the purposes of this exercise, we are assuming that a PDF of a signed policy is a legally binding contract. It goes something like this:

1. CPM drafts the policy in Microsoft Word format and saves it into the insurance company shared drive, or the special software that the company uses (first version of policy).
2. CPM prints it out and gets the legal adviser to sign it (second version of policy).
3. CPM scans it back into the company shared drive/system as a PDF (second copy of second version of policy).
4. CPM drafts a simple covering e-mail with a request for the customer to sign and return the policy (first e-mail), which CPM sends to the customer, attaching the PDF of the policy (third copy of second version of policy).
5. Customer receives the e-mail in their private e-mail system (second copy of first e-mail), prints out the policy and signs it (final version of policy).
6. Customer scans the policy (second copy of final version of policy) and saves it as a PDF on hard drive at home.
7. Customer drafts a letter to CPM, saves it on hard drive (first version of first letter).
8. Customer prints out the letter and signs it (final version of first letter) and posts it to CPM with the policy.
9. Customer also prints out a copy of the final policy for insurance file (third copy of final version of policy).
10. CPM receives the letter and the final version of the policy and scans them both into the company system as PDFs (third copy of final version of policy; second copy of final version of first letter) before filing them.

What can we learn from this exercise?

- there are many steps (at least 10)
- there are different types of record (letter, e-mail and policy)
- there are several versions before the final record (the third version of the policy is the final one)
- both parties keep a copy of the final policy (the customer has paper format and the company has digital format)
- it is not entirely clear which is the master policy, since the CPM scans the final version of the policy into the company system at step 10.

Most importantly, in terms of efficient filing, the CPM needs only the PDF version of the final policy in the company system. Similarly, the customer needs only to keep his PDF or the paper copy.

We have not even touched on the legal adviser's or finance department's filing process. Even this simplified process is quite complicated but note also that many of the documents are ephemeral.

Preliminary decisions

Before we examine filing systems in detail, let's look at some fundamental issues that affect how records are created and relate to each other and some decisions that need to be made before they can be comprehensively and effectively organized.

As we know, records can be created (or received) in different formats – for example digital or paper – but can also be created in different digital formats – for example e-mail or Word for correspondence. It is likely that the body of documentation to record an event, project or issue will not be in one format alone. Rather part will be in paper and part digital. It will not be possible to eliminate this diversity of media and so it is best to broadly map paper and digital classification schemes, because it is much easier for users to follow a parallel logic. It is also best to retain 'born digital' records (those created on computers) in digital format. Avoid duplication of documents across paper and digital systems. Unless there is a requirement to keep records in hard copy format, don't file paper because this duplicates both records and work process.

Remember that the only records that might need to be retained in hard copy are those received into the organization from outside and those that legally need to be kept as such (for example because of seals). Paper 'convenience' copies of digital records need not be totally outlawed, it is just important that they are not filed back into the paper system. Thus one preliminary decision is to what extent the paper and digital systems will complement each other and whether there is a real need for duplication.

Another important preliminary decision is to specify the repositories (and for paper records, container types) in which the records will be kept. The main options are:

- traditional vertical or lateral filing cabinets consisting of drawers with hanging files
- shelves for box files
- dedicated shared drives for the team using the records
- digital records management software systems.

In larger organizations people tend to work in teams, but also need to have places to share records across the teams – for example the HR department might want to consult some staff in developing manuals and policies and later on all staff will need to have access to the final documents. It is then necessary, in addition to deciding on formats, to have a clear list of the places together with guidance on what kind of records to save in each place.

Aims of filing

The aims of filing are simple and straightforward:

- accurate filing of records in the appropriate file, in the correct order
- accurate and appropriate allocation of cross-references
- elimination of unnecessary duplication
- regular filing of records so that no backlog is allowed to accrue
- closure of files that are no longer current or too big
- opening new files for new classification categories, new cases and additional volumes of large files
- tracking of files that are removed from the filing system.

Filing requires documents relating to the same case or transaction to be placed on the same file, and to group files together according to the activity or function that the records are arising from according to classification schemes. The maintenance of the filing system becomes more complicated when there are enough documents in the file to render it physically unwieldy or difficult to navigate and locate relevant records efficiently. One solution to this can be to break the file into volumes on a chronological basis, another is to develop a more hierarchical system. For example, the file of a major customer may be broken down into sub-sections based on types of transaction.

Cross-referencing

Cross-referencing is referring from one file, where the records might be expected to be, to another file where they actually are. For example a letter from a customer expressing satisfaction with a product or service is relevant to the customer file, but may also be used for marketing purposes and also be noted on the files of staff involved in delivering the service. Depending on business needs, the letter might be copied and filed in all three places, or it might be filed on the customer file and cross-referenced from the other two files. In practice, if the cross-reference is for a one-sheet memo it is probably as quick to copy it and file it on the other files. If it were a bulky report, filing a cross-reference sheet on the relevant files would be more appropriate and efficient. Obviously, with digital records, depending on the system functionality, a link can be used as a cross-reference.

Inside the file cover

Records are usually added to files in chronological order – the most recent record appearing at the top or front of the file. Sometimes a file will be divided into subsections according to theme or type of document. This can be useful for smaller operations where initiating new file series is not practical or necessary, or where the working practice requires the records to be categorized but kept together. For example, a current training file relates to a particular type of training course which is run regularly. It is divided into accommodation, action points, ideas to develop for future courses, etc. None of the subsections is large enough to warrant enclosing in its own folder and it is more convenient to have it all together in one file. Another reason for this approach to filing is when some of the documentation is more important than another. For example, policy and contract documents need to be kept longer and be easily accessible, whereas routine correspondence quickly ceases to be relevant. Other documentation might need to be separated out because it gets regularly updated, as is the case with guidance notes, for example.

Filing and sharing practices for digital records

In the digital environment people can be reluctant to save their records in shared areas because some records should have limited access or they fear colleagues will change them or inadvertently delete them. An electronic records management system can be configured to prevent this happening, because it will assign authority to access records, as well as to delete them. Moreover, records cannot be changed: if a change needs to be made the record is saved as a different record. Even without an ERMS (see below), systems can be configured to ensure restricted access to sensitive records that need to be shared, assigning read-only values to prevent changes and institute regular back-ups to allow recovery of deleted records.

The digital era has brought many possibilities for filing and managing records to become more efficient, eliminate some of the drudgery of keeping them organized and accessible and enable this information asset to be more fully exploited. It is no longer necessary to laboriously create file lists and/or index cards to manage, track and retrieve records – there is document name searching, full text retrieval and database functionality to help.

> **Electronic records management system (ERMS):** software program for creating, capturing, managing, sharing, setting retention values for and deleting digital records. Also capable of handling metadata for paper records.

There are also electronic records management systems (ERMS) specially developed to manage records – some of them comply with standards such as the US Department of Defense standard on electronic records management software (5015.02) and ICA-Req, both of which specify the functionality necessary for managing records in electronic records management systems. Microsoft Sharepoint can also be used to manage records. However, the success of the technology in managing the records depends enormously on the human beings using it, and the recordkeeping systems which they devise. The technology cannot decide how to configure classification schemes or which folders records need to be assigned to.

Successful implementation of an ERMS, or configuring Sharepoint to manage records, requires a lot of resource at the beginning. An organization-wide file plan usually needs to be developed and agreed by all users, retention schedules need to be created and access authorities specified and assigned. Because it affects all users in an organization there is usually a pilot phase, followed by roll-out, when all users are expected to adopt it. It is always a big change for end-users and managing that change is very challenging for organizations. Many organizations have failed to implement ERMSs successfully. The opportunities offered by this technology for managing records are boundless, but the need for solid records management expertise and for end-users to take the time to work on file plans and retention schedules is crucial to successful implementation. Chapter 3 will cover specifying and implementing electronic records management system software in more detail.

Many organizations have no possibility of procuring an ERMS, because of the software costs and resources required to implement and run them. However, as already indicated, the success of recordkeeping systems does not solely depend on having dedicated software. The expertise of the records manager who develops and implements it, the quality of the initial training for users, users' adherence to the guidelines and ongoing maintenance are equally important factors. Checklist 2.2 gives tips for achieving a high standard of records management for current records in an existing technology environment.

Checklist 2.2 Managing current digital records

- Work with the team or department.
- Identify different drives, mobile and storage devices where records are kept.
- Get around a table together to look at a large, projected view of the computer drive(s).
- Look at the existing folder structure and decide what works and what doesn't work. Things to look for include:
  - folders with titles which are colleagues' (or ex-colleagues') names
  - folders with different names but containing records that support the same activity, case, etc.
  - lots of loose documents in folders which have sub-folders
  - legacy folders left over from previous colleagues or previous parts or incarnations of the team/department

  - folders and documents which are no longer accessed.
- Decide as a team about the right structure and practices for recordkeeping, including:
  - rules for what records should be saved to which drives (tip: almost everything should be in the shared area)
  - the best folder structure and rules for use
  - where to put folders and documents that are no longer current
  - how to sort out any legacy folders
  - who will take responsibility for monitoring the shared drive to ensure it remains organized going forwards.
- Document the decisions made about managing records, re-organize the records as agreed.

Classification

> 'Classification is the process of devising and applying schemes based on the business activities which generate records, whereby they are categorised in systematic and consistent ways to facilitate their capture, retrieval, maintenance and disposal. Classification includes determining document or filing name conventions, user permissions and security restrictions on records.'
>
> AS 4390.1-1996 Part 1

Probably the classification scheme we are all most familiar with is the one used in libraries, the Dewey Decimal System, which classifies books according to subject. Another one is found in grocery stores or in the online shop, where food and household goods are categorized according to the way they need to be kept – chilled, frozen or store cupboard. For the purposes of filing systems, classification is the process by which records of an organization are grouped into units which reflect the work of the organization or team and provide the complete picture with context of the activity, case or business. It should ideally be function-based, but sometimes it will reflect subjects.

Schemes and hierarchies

Table 2.2 gives some options for organizing records.

Before we go any further, let's have a look at the ways in which files are created and how that influences the kind of system they need. A subject file arises where you have areas of interest or activity that can be best linked by the subject. For example in a politician's filing system, he may have files relating to things like tobacco and smoking, boxing and bicycle helmets in a

Table 2.2 *Organizing records and files*

Type of file	Arrangement of files within series	Arrangement of records on the file
• project	• by project title	• chronological • consecutively according to reference numbers • alphabetical
• customer	• by customer name	
• invoices and receipts	• by tax year	
• board meetings	• by meeting date	
• students	• by student name	
• marketing	• by campaign	
• property development	• by property title	

subject file series covering a wide range of subjects that may be campaign or parliamentary issues. A case file is a file that relates to a specific name – of a person, subject, action, event, etc. Case file series tend to generate many files which are inherently similar in content. Examples are insurance files for policy holders, personnel files for employees and medical records for patients. Figure 2.2 explains record classification hierarchies.

- Hierarchies are necessary in classification schemes when the work of the team or department is complex.
- If the team only deals with a simple activity, such as managing customers with insurance policies, the files form a single set (also known as a record series) of case records.
- If the team has a number of more complex activities, for example a human resources department managing recruitment, current staff and training, the filing structure needs to be hierarchical.

Figure 2.2 *Record classification hierarchies*

Classification schemes can be quite simple, consisting of a list of files in alphabetical or numerical order, but often they are more complex and reflect a hierarchy of over-arching functions and the activities into which they are divided. Figure 2.3 gives an example of the hierarchy of an HR filing system which shows this.

Function	• Human Resources Management
Activity	– Recruitment
File	† Post title
Records	‡ Advertisement
•	‡ Applications
	‡ Interview schedule

Figure 2.3 *Example of a human resources file classification*

Figure 2.4 gives an example of how project files might be classified, showing how the difference in the amount of funding requires different management as is reflected in the different filing hierarchies.

- Projects under £1 million
  - Gate house redecoration
  - Number 53 Mill Lane roof repairs
- Projects over £1 million
  - Tower construction project (Project ref/no. XXX)
    - † Contracts
      - ‡ Rejected tenders
      - ‡ Successful tender and final contract
    - † Correspondence
    - † Finance
      - ‡ Budget
      - ‡ Expenditure
    - † Plans
      - ‡ Draft
      - ‡ Final as built (note CAD version located at: xxx)

Figure 2.4 *Example of a project file classification scheme*

With digital records an additional level is advisable to divide the records by date, for example 'Budgets 2010'. This will facilitate the quick deletion of all 2010 budget files, thus eliminating review of all budget files to find 2010 documents. Following simple naming conventions, such as ordering the title first by date, will ensure that the folders sort in accordance with retention requirements.

How to classify your documents and other files

How do we decide on the rules for grouping individual records together? Mostly it will be obvious to those who are doing the work and recordkeeping professionals who know how to review existing systems and analyse the work process and activities. Table 2.3 provides some different options for classifying records.

When developing classification schemes, it is also a good idea to separate policy files from operational files and reference material from records

Table 2.3 *Ways to classify records*

Types of information	Definition	Examples
Organizational	Information which mirrors organization structures	• by section – Recruitment team • by department – HR department • by country – USA • by region – Latin America and the Caribbean region
Functional	According to the activity or function which the information is created by or supports	• High level – HR management • Low level – recruitment management • Working groups – staff satisfaction group • Project groups – second floor refurbishment
Subject	Information grouped to reflect areas of interest	• Country files • Areas of professional expertise • Training opportunities

providing evidence of and supporting the work. If, when it comes to looking at the contents of the file, it has a lot of subcategories and/or is getting really bulky, it may mean you need a more detailed hierarchical structure.

Once the classification scheme is developed and approved, it acts like a pick-list of options for placing files in the hierarchy. It should be possible to classify all records into the scheme. Where it is not possible, provided the scheme is being used properly, this indicates there is a need to add in a category. This is often due to additional functions and activities being taken on by the team. The reason functional classification schemes are often best is that new sections are easy to add – and if there are reorganizations that result in team mergers or teams losing areas of work, it is easy to join or split the classification schemes. If the classification scheme is clear and detailed enough, it should be possible to easily extract file series to move to new teams.

In addition to the classification scheme, filing systems also need classification procedures in order to ensure that it is being used properly. These need to include:

- how to use the classification scheme and to open or close files
- who has the authority to make changes or update the scheme
- how to add or remove classification categories.

The terminology used in the classification scheme, together with the file (and in the digital arena, the document) titles are an inherent part of classification. Without clear and consistent document, file and category titles a classification scheme cannot be used. In paper systems the folder labels need to be clearly written. All these elements together ensure that end-users understand quickly what they are looking at and where any record should be found. The next sub-section covers good file naming practice.

File naming

As mentioned above, another crucial aspect of filing systems is file naming, or labelling – what the documents, records, files and file categories should be called. One key issue is that different people might call the same topic, function or category different things or might construct a file title differently. Figure 2.5 discusses the issues to consider.

Another important issue is deciding what kind of labelling system to use, for example full titles, acronyms, numeric or alpha-numeric. Here are the three main options together with some tips on their benefits and disadvantages:

1. **Alphabetical:** instantly recognizable, keep file names short, need to ensure agreed preferred terms are part of documentation, also agree ordering of elements in title (e.g., surname, first name).
2. **Alpha-numeric:** flexible, easy to add sections into classification scheme, use of letters can help people remember type of file/file names, can be time-consuming to do labelling and coding.
3. **Numeric:** simpler and faster than text-based labels, requires index or key, less recognizable than letters or words.

Scenario:
A project to develop a property has a plot number, a property title and a popular name. The file of records relating to the project could be given any one of several names:

- P104
- Thyme Artspace
- Waterman's Sweet Factory.

1. What is the best way to deal with this in the classification scheme?
2. What will happen if this is not dealt with?

Solution:
1. Name the file(s) according to the official file title and include the alternatives with a cross-reference to the official file.
2. If this is not dealt with in the classification scheme and filing procedures there is a danger that there will be three incomplete files dealing with the same property.

Figure 2.5 *Deciding file names*

Controlled language

Controlled language can be useful in developing file naming conventions. It gives a preferred term, offering a way of identifying the different options when a file or category might be labelled more than one way. This makes it easier both to decide where to file things and where to find them, but it also ensures that there are no duplicate files covering the same case or issue. As a result the person looking for records can be confident that they have found all the relevant records. The non-preferred terms are documented in the controlled language so someone looking for the case or issues under one of the other names would find a cross-reference to the relevant file. An example might be that the files relating to 'ornaments' are in fact called 'decorations'. In a controlled language there would be an entry for 'decorations', which is known as the preferred term. There would also be an entry for 'ornaments' but the user would be directed to see or use 'decorations'.

Version identification

Document titles may need to include version information. It is possible in the digital world to set up and find this information in the document properties or other embedded metadata. However, including it in the document name makes it quicker and easier for everyone to know the most recent version. There are several options for identifying versions. Some organizations use words – for example preliminary, intermediary, final. Another option is to use v (for version) and a number – hence the first version is v1. When the document is updated, it is saved with the same name but the next consecutive number.

Naming conventions

Naming conventions are rules that govern the choice of file and folder titles and how the various parts of the title are ordered. They allow all people using the filing system to easily identify files for filing and retrieval purposes. The document name should answer two questions without needing to open the document itself: what is this document and is it the one I am looking for? Document and folder or file names can be made up of a number of different elements. Table 2.4 gives the main ones to consider:

Table 2.4 *Elements of document names*

Element	Recommendations	Example
Organizational structure	Put in reverse hierarchical order	Recruitment HR
Dates	Always structure in year, month, day order and use numbers not words for the months so the documents will sort chronologically	2016-01-17
Document types	Use standard terms and make document type the final element in the name	Policy, plan, guideline
Names	Always put the surname first	Smith, John; Mills, Louisa
Program	It is not necessary to include this as systems usually assign it automatically	

In deciding what order to put the different elements of the name in, combine them to give the most useful information first. For example: Company Merger-Boss-Master Plan (topic – recipient – document type). Document names that include all the desired elements may get very long. If the specific element comes first, the part of the name visible in the display box should enable the files to be identified and located. However, if it is difficult to locate files because of the length of the name and the number of documents in the folder, consideration should be given to sub-dividing the folder. It is not good practice to use forward slashes in document names in Microsoft Office because the computer mistakes them for file paths. Similarly the use of full stops can be confused with the program extension in some older versions of Microsoft Windows. Hyphens can be a good replacement.

Generally speaking, document names should not repeat elements which are already included in the folder name. However this requirement, based on a need to keep the title short, must be balanced against the need to include enough information to identify documents if they become detached from the folder. It may also be necessary to rename some documents if they are moved to shared folders or to the intranet.

It can be useful to put some of the elements of the document title into the document itself, for example in the footer. Using the Microsoft Office feature that automatically inserts the document path into the document easily allows others to locate both digital and paper record iterations.

Filing documentation and guidelines

However good the filing system is, in order for it to be successfully implemented and work well, it needs to be documented and to be operated by staff with some basic training in using and maintaining the system.

What documentation is needed for filing systems?

We have already mentioned all three kinds of documentation needed to underpin good filing practice – whether in the paper, digital or hybrid situation. Table 2.5 gives the content of the documentation and includes a fourth, less crucial piece of documentation, the file list, which may or may not be required, depending on the complexity of the classification scheme, the importance of the records and the nature of the work they support. It also includes the retention schedule, which will be covered in great detail in the next chapter.

Filing guidelines

Although it takes time to work through the different aspects of filing paper and saving digital records into an organized system in an effective and efficient way, it is very important to create filing guidelines to ensure consistency in filing and to support new staff using the system. It can be difficult to convince colleagues that even small, straightforward systems need to be documented, but it is part of good records management practice which contributes to the overall accountability of the organization.

Good filing practices are also crucial to managing records as they move from the current to non-current phase of their lives. This is because retrieval depends on a clear, explicit system of classification and as records become less current it is more difficult to find them from memory rather than a logical system.

Filing systems that work

Having discussed all the aspects that need to be considered in designing a filing system, what are the success factors and how can we ensure the system

Table 2.5 *Filing documentation*

Document	Contents
Classification scheme(s)	• Introduction explaining what it is, how it is organized and why • Full list of file categories • Whether it covers both paper and digital records • How to use the classification scheme
Naming conventions	Details of how to construct and order elements in file names
File lists	Complete list of all files in one or more filing categories
Filing guidelines	Detailed instructions on how to use and manage the filing system including: • who has authority to make changes to the filing system, who does the filing, who uses the files • security procedures – such as locking filing cabinets, instructions for keeping files secure outside of the cabinets, protection of mobile devices outside the office environment and password and encryption policy • rules for deciding whether the record should be kept in paper or digital format • what records to keep in which part of the network, depending on the level of security and shared access • identifying the file to which a record belongs • physical aspects of filing such as hole punching, where to write labels, how sections may be separated within the file • in what order to place records on files • detailed instructions about cross-referencing – when, how and when not to • what material should not be filed • how to decide in which category a file/folder belongs • how to add a new item to the classification scheme • how to rename an item in the classification scheme • how to order the files within the classification category • when and how to close a file and open a new volume • when to create a new file • when to close down a file and what to do with it • how to retrieve files • how to return retrieved files.
Retention schedules	List of file series giving length of time to be retained before destruction/deletion or transfer to the archives

will work? The design of the system is obviously crucial. Checklist 2.3 provides some basic criteria.

Checklist 2.3 Criteria for successful filing systems

- The classification scheme and folder structures reflect and support the organization's business functions and activities.
- File titles, folder and document names accurately reflect the contents.

- The classification scheme (or file plan) and file lists are easy to use.
- Physical movement of files is tracked so that they can always be located when needed.
- Clear and simple procedures for using the systems, well publicized and enforced.
- Users are trained to understand the system and follow procedures.
- Closed files and folders are regularly removed from the system to prevent congestion.
- Systems are regularly reviewed to ensure business needs continue to be met.

As hinted in the last sub-section, much depends on ensuring that users are given adequate training and have guidance to refer to. It is also really important to have someone who takes responsibility for being the file monitor. This entails periodically checking the paper and digital filing repositories and ensuring that:

- the physical organization of the paper files or digital folder structure is in good order
- there are no empty folders or categories
- files are generally in the right order
- digital document and folder names and file titles are properly constructed
- there are no paper records sitting around waiting to be filed
- there are no loose digital documents in the higher level folders
- there are no duplicate or ephemeral items in files and folders.

The same person should also be responsible for training new team members and reminding existing colleagues of how to operate the system.

Regular review is also important to ensure the system remains effective and fit for purpose. Like all other aspects of records management, filing systems need reviewing to ensure they are working well and remain fit for purpose. New systems require an initial review after about a year. Thereafter once every couple of years should be enough, unless there are obvious problems. Reviews can be carried out in the same way that the work, records and existing records were examined and analysed prior to setting up the system.

Use and tracking

'Tracking of the movement and use of records within a records system is required to:

(a) identify outstanding action required,

(b) enable retrieval of a record,
(c) prevent loss of records,
(d) monitor usage for systems maintenance and security, and maintain an auditable trail of records transactions (i.e. capture or registration, classification, indexing, storage, access and use, migration and disposition), and
(e) maintain capacity to identify the operational origins of individual records where systems have been amalgamated or migrated.'

ISO 15489-1:2001

Current recordkeeping systems will, by their nature, be frequently accessed and used. The files or digital folders will be used for a variety of reasons by team members and be constantly added to over time. The activity of accessing records in the filing system needs to be subject to some general rules as well as monitoring, since otherwise there is a risk that records may be lost, changed or misfiled.

Why track files?

Files are tracked:

- to monitor and ensure actions are taken
- to prevent loss of records
- to maintain security
- to manage current storage needs.

For paper systems, tracking the use – and location – of files is dependent on having a system that all staff follow. This can be done with cards that are placed in the hanging file (or in holders in place of the box files) so that anyone looking for the file can see that it is out and who is using it. The card would act as a form list so that users can document the pertinent information, for example their name, extension number and the file details. Cards can be re-usable for any file or attached to a specific file. In the latter case, it is then possible to build up an audit trail of activity on the file. Figure 2.6 gives a fictional example.

Date	Removed by	Extension number	File title	Reason for removing file
13/11/2013	Fred Jones	7215	DH Crown	Filed draft policy
2nd Dec	Rob McDonald	7253	DH Crown	Added signed policy
2/12/2013	Ruby Green	7235	DH Crown	Random file check
15th Jan 2014	Rob McDonald	7253	DH Crown	Added insurance claim form

Figure 2.6 *The Insurance Company Ltd file tracking card*

In the electronic environment, as we have seen above, there are two main scenarios: a dedicated ERMS or the existing (usually Microsoft) platform. With an ERMS it is possible to have an audit trail of who has accessed the records, and if one individual is working on a document, no one else can edit it at the same time (although this should apply only to documents in draft). With the standard Microsoft Office setup it is more difficult to keep track of who accesses documents, unless the document properties defaults are carefully tailored.

Security

Security for current record systems is important for a number of reasons. Ensuring that records are kept securely and that only those authorized to create, manage and access them can do so is crucial to confidence that the records are reliable. If the records are not kept at a standard of security that ensures they cannot be changed or removed without due authorization, there can be neither accountability nor confidence in the function.

How can we keep records secure?

We keep records secure by implementing:

- appropriate levels of security assigned to record groups depending on sensitivity of work and content
- individual usernames
- good password practice, regularly changed, never shared
- encrypted mobile devices and record storage media
- locked filing cabinets and/or file rooms
- clear desk policy
- effective staff training and regular awareness raising.

Security classification

In most organizations, there will be records with differing sensitivity. The sensitivity will depend on factors such as commercial confidentiality, maturity of research, national security, or whether the records contain personal data. It may be necessary to implement a formal security policy and classification scheme, as happens in many governments and international organizations. Figure 2.7 gives information about the US classification system.

To operate a more formal record security classification scheme, the following elements are necessary:

- a set of classification categories and markings, together with a clear description of what kind of material each category covers
- rules as to the application of markings
- documented procedures for handling information in each category, including when information is in transit
- de-classification and re-classification procedures.

According to Executive Order 13526 (2009):

- There are three levels of classification:
  - **Top Secret:** for information which if disclosed would cause 'exceptionally grave damage' to national security
  - **Secret:** for information which, if disclosed would cause 'serious damage' to national security
  - **Confidential:** for information that would 'damage' national security if publicly disclosed
- Access to classified information depends on Government security clearance
- There is no need to classify records unless 'unauthorized disclosure could reasonably be expected to cause identifiable or describable damage to the national security'
- 'Unclassified' is not a security level but rather the default position for information that can be accessed by/released to people who don't have security clearance

Figure 2.7 *US Government Security Classification*[1]

Implementing a system like this will ensure that staff can share or withhold information confident that they are complying with organizational – and legal – requirements. In organizations which are covered by Freedom of Information legislation, there is also the consideration that all records may potentially have to be disclosed. A clear and transparent security classification scheme can therefore also be crucial to the disclosure process, because it will mark up only the records where there is a sensitivity issue, which are the ones where access requests may need to be challenged under legal exemptions.

However, most organizations can operate less stringent systems which consist of ensuring there is a policy and implementation guidance to help staff recognize records containing sensitive information and ensure they are maintained and protected with appropriate security levels. For both formal and less formal systems, documentation in the form of policy and guidelines, together with staff training, is vital to ensure the scheme will work.

Personal data

Personal data: any information, in any format, which allows an individual to be recognized. For most people this requires a name and another piece of identifying information such as an address or date of birth.

Personal data needs to be identified and kept securely by the people who need the data to carry out the activity for which it was originally collected (or given). It is very surprising how much personal data – of staff, customers and stakeholders – organizations gather without being aware of the nature of the information and the special management it requires. Some data is not just personal, but sensitive personal data about factors like health, income, or ethnicity, and it may not be appropriate to keep it. Current filing systems need to be able to recognize and handle personal records with similar safety mechanisms to the ones for security-classified records discussed above. Retention of personal data will be covered in the records management section.

Password protection

Why are passwords like underwear?

- They should be mysterious.
- You shouldn't share them with others.
- Longer is better.
- They have to be changed regularly.
- You shouldn't show them off.
- You need a few of them.

We all know what to do, don't we? We should use strong passwords that are a combination of lower and upper case letters, numbers and special characters that are not a string as appears on the keyboard, a word in the dictionary or the name of your pet or little girl. They should be at least 8 digits long and you should have a different one for every application. As if that were not enough to deal with, you should change them all often.

Many organizations have IT system set-ups that make staff change their passwords regularly, do not allow them to repeat passwords on a cycle, and do not allow weak passwords. Similarly, many consumer sites periodically require customers to change their passwords. If this seems a time-consuming and onerous task, it is worth remembering the risks associated with weak passwords:

- loss of information
- information tampering and misuse
- loss of income
- loss of life (depending on the nature of the business and the nature of the organization)
- loss of credibility and reputation
- dismissal from employment

- fines or imprisonment
- loss of friends and hassle from the family.

Encryption

Encryption is another way to prevent unauthorized use of information and records. It is a very ancient process which modern technology has impacted in two main ways. The first is in the ability to use complicated algorithms to generate the code to lock and unlock encrypted information. The other is in the invention of the public and private key algorithm. Previously encryption codes needed to be shared between two individuals – and only two individuals – and their security depended on there being safe communication between the two parties. With public/private keys, it is possible for the public key of an individual to be used by anyone else to encrypt something which only that individual's private key can decrypt.

Encryption does not necessarily stop hacking, theft or unauthorized access to records, but it prevents the thief or hacker from being able to understand the information in the records.

Mobile devices and storage media

Mobile devices, such as laptops, smartphones and tablets, and storage media such as USB sticks are very convenient for creating, transferring, accessing and generally supporting work when staff are travelling or working from home. The records on these devices are very vulnerable, since the hardware itself is very portable (which is why they are so popular) and very easily left behind or lost. There are a number of ways to protect the records, such as strong passwords and encryption keys, but records held in this way will always be at risk. Guidance for staff should make the risks clear and outline their responsibilities with respect to passwords and encryption of sensitive and restricted information. Guidelines should also cover basic theft prevention measures, such as not leaving devices and bags unattended even in locked cars.

Clear desk policies

A clear desk policy, where staff are not permitted to leave records and files lying around on their desks overnight, is a good basic security measure. It reduces risk of theft and of unauthorized access, as well as being a basic protective measure in case of fire or flood, since drawers and boxes provide a first line of defence that will hold for a period of time. Password-protected screen savers that kick in after a few minutes perform a similar function for digital records.

Staff training and awareness

In order for security measures and controls to be effective, staff need to be aware of the security issues and ways to protect records, both within the organization and outside. Security policy and procedures are always a fine balancing act between ensuring safety and hindering productivity, so taking into account the views and suggestions of staff working with the records is always important.

Successful implementation of record and information security protocols requires regular staff awareness campaigns and effective baseline training for all staff. At some point it may also require penalties – if there is no consequence to breaching security protocols, the whole system is undermined. The records management team will need to work closely with the IT team to develop effective protocols.

Vital records in offices

> **Vital records:** those records which are critical to reconstituting the information assets of an organization in the event of a disaster. Such records enable the organization to set up a new base, continue conducting business, access other assets and defend itself from and by legal action.

Disaster prevention and emergency recovery will be addressed in the records management section. However, because vital records are often only vital whilst they are current, and it is end-users who create and manage them, vital records management needs to be part of the overall current records management procedures. Vital records are those records an organization needs to continue to operate its business during and following an emergency. The vital records programme enables those records identified and protected as vital records to be immediately available in the event of a disaster. Figure 2.8 sets out the main components.

A policy, set of procedures and documentation to protect vital records and ensure they are available in the event of a disaster. This involves:

- identification of business processes and assets that are crucial to running the business, particularly those that may be regularly or immediately deployed
- identification of those records which are vital to running business, defending and accessing assets, legal standing and future planned growth
- compiling a list to support their protection and management over time, including replacement with current versions as frequently as necessary
- instituting strategies for protection (for example sending copies offsite)
- developing plans to recover vital records in the event of an emergency and training personnel for likely scenarios.

Figure 2.8 *The vital records programme*

Identifying vital records

Identifying vital records can be tricky, because it depends on several factors. First of all there needs to be an overview of the organization, its functions and the records that support it. Secondly, senior level staff need to engage with the process of identifying the vital functions and activities to ensure that the correct records are prioritized. Finally, it is necessary to involve record creators or users in identifying vital records, but it can be difficult to tactfully explain to them that all their records (even if they can't do their jobs without them) are not vital in the event of an emergency.

It can also help to view vital records as the records needed to ensure the organization can resume business, rather than all the records necessary to keep the business running over time. For example, in the event of a disaster it is vital to access staff contact details to ensure their safety, ask them to come into the (existing or new) workplace or to tell them to remain at home for the time being. It is not necessary to have all of the staff personnel files in the immediate aftermath of a disaster, but it is important to have them in the mid to long term. Essentially, it is the difference between keeping the organization operational and enabling the long-term recovery of the whole organization, not just vital functions.

The vital records list should be based on a list of vital functions agreed by senior management who understand the mission-critical operations, fundamental responsibilities and essential activities of the organization. It should be drawn up by or at least developed in consultation with the records manager and/or archivist because of their knowledge of the relationship between functions and records. End-users will also need to be consulted. It should be reviewed by the legal adviser, IT team and senior management. Checklist 2.4 gives some pointers as to which records are vital.

Checklist 2.4 Vital records criteria

The precise set of vital records that need protection in case of a disaster will depend on the organization – its status, its business, the way it operates and its culture. However, there are some general guidelines to follow:

- Financial records proving payment or monies owed to the organization
- Employee contact information and ongoing obligations such as payroll and benefits
- Records which fulfil legal and government requirements, allowing the organization to operate within the law, protect itself and/or individuals, and protect against litigation
- Manufacturing records such as production specifications, inventory lists, current research and development, licences to operate

- Insurance policy information
- Ownership records for property, patents and trademarks, registration numbers, franchise information, capital investments
- Major contracts and agreements
- Corporate records such as minutes of directors meetings, incorporation papers, organization charts
- Core operational records such as case files, membership records etc.
- Facility records providing information on location, plans and operation of buildings, entrances, safes, sprinkler and heat and air con systems, alarm systems, security systems.

It is important to bear in mind that only a very small proportion of an organization's records are likely to be vital – between 2 and 4%. Vital records are generally current, supporting and documenting the ongoing business of the organization. Records designated as vital will need special management which is resource-intensive. It is therefore really important to correctly identify vital records.

Protection strategies

Vital records need to be protected but also accessible in the event of an emergency, even if access to the organization's premises is not possible. Apart from the organization's overall disaster prevention strategy, there are three main ways of protecting vital records:

1. Copying them and sending them offsite. The copies can be in the same medium or a different one. However, it may be necessary to have the original master of some vital records (for example deeds, contracts, and articles of incorporation) for legal reasons. In this case the best protection is in a fire-proof safe with an attested copy as a back-up at another site.
2. Keeping them on-site in enhanced protection (for example a fire-proof safe).
3. Relying on dispersal – where copies are sent to branch offices because of routine business needs.

Option 3 is probably the least effective, but it might be the most cost-effective. A small archives and records management consultancy with two partners and no staff, having considered the likely disasters and the impact on the business, might decide that the routine transfer of operational and project documentation and the exchange and copying-in of e-mails between partners in separate locations is an adequate risk mitigation strategy.

Option 2, keeping vital records on-site in a fire-proof safe, carries the risk of the safe exploding or being buried in certain kinds of disasters – as well as the onus of ensuring that vital records are always deposited and/or returned when used.

Option 1, sending copies off-site is probably the best strategy but it requires careful management with a resource implication. There needs to be a suitable site (which may or may not be owned by the organization) and records need to be copied and sent there promptly and regularly. Older records which have been superseded either by more current records or by changes in the business need to be pulled and destroyed regularly. There needs to be procedures for recovering the copies in the event of a disaster to ensure they are available to the business wherever it ends up operating.

More and more of organizations' records – and therefore the vital records – are being created and managed in computer systems. On the one hand this is good news for vital records, because it is easy to copy them – indeed, back-up procedures are routine in most organizations as a contingency for even small information losses. On the other hand, it is easy for the vital records (2–4% of all the records) to be unidentifiable and inseparable from all the other data on the back-up tapes. It is therefore important to have a system where vital records are easily flagged and recovered from the back-ups in the event of a disaster. It is even better to have a dedicated back-up system for vital records. For paper records it will be necessary to consider the benefits, costs and potential disadvantages of copying them – to paper, microform or digital format.

Vital records copied in digital formats need to be accessible in the event of a disaster and so it is important to have contingency plans to access computer equipment, software (including documentation as necessary) and a power supply. For vital records that are not so current, you need to be sure they can still be accessed and read on more recent hardware with later versions of software.

Procedures will be needed to manage the vital records protection strategy. In addition to the vital records list, they should include:

- who makes the copies in which formats
- how often (or on what cycle) copies are made
- what to do with the copy to get it off-site, or otherwise protect it
- how to document records sent off-site and maintaining an overall inventory of off-site vital records accessible in the event of an emergency
- what to do with expired vital records
- how to recover and reconstitute vital records.

Security procedures are needed to ensure that the records are safe while in transit and at the off-site location.

Round-up

Current records management is more dependent on end-users than most other aspects of records management. It is therefore an area where it is most difficult for recordkeeping professionals to establish control. However, end-users are often grateful for advice and help in setting up systems that work for them. As we have seen in this section, the creation of records and the way they are organized, maintained and protected are crucial to the quality, accessibility and reliability of the body of records as a whole.

Note

1 www.whitehouse.gov/the-press-office/executive-order-classified-national-security-information.

CHAPTER 3
Records management

Introduction

> '[Records management is] the field of management responsible for the efficient and systematic control of the creation, receipt, maintenance, use and disposition of records, including processes for capturing and maintaining evidence of and information about business activities and transactions in the form of records.'
>
> ISO 15489-1:2001 (E) Information and documentation – Records management – Part 1: general

Chapter 1 defined records management as 'a comprehensive regime which controls records through their lifecycle, including: deciding what records to create; organizing them so that they support business needs and authorized retrieval; evaluating and imposing retention requirements; documented destruction or designation as archives'. I think of records management as encompassing everything that happens to records from the point that someone conceives the need to document something to the point that record is destroyed – and if it is not destroyed it continues to be managed as an archival record indefinitely. However, as this book makes a distinction between the main phases of the lifecycle broadly based on currency and custodianship, this chapter deals with what happens when records are no longer needed constantly for current business purposes to support the operational work of end-users. It is at this stage that records managers – professionals whose main function is concerned with managing records effectively – usually get custody of the records, or at least get involved. The next chapter deals with managing archives, which requires a different set of skills (sometimes from a different individual) and different storage facilities, to look after records which need to be kept indefinitely for reasons separate from immediate business needs.

Records lifecycle: a metaphor to describe the existence span of records, divided into stages to reflect the different processes needed to manage them.

According to our Chapter 1 definition, records are: 'recorded information in any media or format, providing reliable evidence of human activity'. Thus, records management is exactly what the term implies: managing records. It is about control, about knowing what records the organization needs and creates as well as making sure the records are organized effectively. Moreover, it is about understanding what the organization does and which records arise from its functions and activities. We noted earlier this link between activity and record: records arise from work, rather than the work aim being to create records. Knowing these things, we can decide the best way to organize the records so that they can be stored efficiently, found if required and destroyed when no longer needed. We can also ensure that the records which would be most vital in the event of a disaster are identified and protected or backed up in such a way that they can be recalled immediately. Although this all reads as a fairly simple exercise, records management is a function which breaks down into a surprisingly large number of activities. We will cover them all in this chapter, following the record's journey via a series of processes and sub-systems.

Information management

Information: conveyed or represented fact or opinion which informs overall understanding about something or someone. Not necessarily evidence.

For most of us, all aspects of our lives – working, social and in our interactions with government, healthcare and education – depend on and are saturated with information. This section introduces the concept of information and the distinction between information and records. Since information and records are so frequently confused and can be interchangeable in the way they are used, records managers and archivists must be able to manage information as well as records. Figure 3.1 defines information.

If we refer back to our definition of record ('recorded information in any media or format, providing reliable evidence of human activity'), we can begin to see that some of the information concepts apply.

Information is defined in The International Council on Archives' *Dictionary of Archival Terminology* (2nd Edition, K. G. Sauer, 1988) as 'recorded data', and in the Oxford English Dictionary as 'Items of knowledge or news'. The term is a difficult one to categorically define but there are some concepts and ideas that can help us to do this in the context of managing records. In that context, information is:

- knowledge, data, facts, news
- passed from one party to another
- processed in some way
- interpretation of facts or data
- not fictional
- not necessarily evidence.

Figure 3.1 *What is information?*

Records are not fictional, they are factual, they can contain data and they can be news. On the other hand some of the concepts do not apply: records are definitely evidence and whilst records can transfer knowledge, knowledge itself does not have to be recorded.

Table 3.1 gives some examples of how the bumph we accumulate in everyday life can be categorized as information, records or archives (remembering the definition of archives as 'records . . . selected for permanent preservation').

Table 3.1 *Information, record or archive?*

Example	Information	Record	Archive
Birth certificate	✓	✓	✓
Current driving licence	✓	✓	×
Textbook on archives and records management	✓	×	×
Newspaper cutting	✓	×	×
Advert for double glazing	✓	×	×
Minutes of parent–teacher association	✓	? only if the person keeping the minutes is the official custodian	If the minutes are records, then they will be archival
Print-out from website	✓	×	×
Personal address book	✓	✓	×
File of recipes taken from magazines, copied from books, collected from friends	✓	×	×
Scrapbook of holiday memorabilia	✓	✓	✓This might be considered personal archives
Encyclopaedia	✓	×	×

This demonstrates several things:

- all archives are records but not all records are archives (as we established in Chapter 1)
- all records and all archives are – or provide – information
- copies of records and archives are more information than record or archive – unless the original is lost
- one person's, team's or organization's records can be another's information
- information can be both contained in records and archives and separate from them even within the same overall system.

It should also be noted that managing information is usually not concerned with the relationships between the separate constituents of the mass of information, but rather about organizing it so it can be found and used later on.

In reality, of course, the distinctions can be more blurred, but there are a couple of questions we can ask to test whether something is a record and determine how we manage it:

1 What is it a record of?
2 Is it a record of our organization?

Managing information alongside records and archives

The creators and users of records will not see such a clear and important distinction between records and information. A good example of the blurred distinction is freedom of, or as it is called in some countries, access to, information legislation. Whilst in general it refers to the information which provides evidence of actions and decisions (records), the term 'information' is generally used rather than 'records' or even 'records and information'. Because of the indistinct boundaries between information and records, it is important for us to be not only aware of the difference, but also to include a certain amount of information management in the scope of our work.

Managing information is about making the distinction between information, records and archives, organizing and maintaining it so that it is accessible when needed by authorized people, is kept current and is eliminated when no longer needed. Obviously in the case of records selected for the archives the aim is to maintain them for ever.

For records management purposes, the goal of information management is to help end-users and gatherers of information to identify it clearly and understand that it has a different value from records. If information and records are mixed, we should help end-users organize the system differently to manage the records more efficiently. Beyond that we can leave them to organize their information as they wish.

Information overload

'Information overload' describes the situation when we have so much information at our disposal that we are unable to process it all. For the end-user that processing usually involves digesting the information to take action or make a recommendation or decision, but for those of us (often of course including end-users) whose goal is to manage records, processing also requires getting control of that information.

One of the main reasons for this overload is the ever-increasing speed at which modern technology is advancing. It affects the computer applications used to support the running of organizations and households which generate and keep records in both the business and private domain. This includes not only desktop and server-based systems but also mobile technology and social media. It follows that this technology supports ever-increasing retrieval, production and distribution of information, including records. As a result, individuals at home and at work constantly need not only to adapt to new ways of working but also to select that which is useful and important from the over-abundance of information. Already in the 1990s studies were suggesting that these pressures resulted in issues such as stress, anxiety, reduced memory, limited attention spans and poor decision-making amongst managers.

Records management is about assigning different values to different types of information to ensure that it is managed appropriately and efficiently. In practising records management, we teach end-users to recognize and even make those distinctions as well as give them the tools and processes to take control of the information that surrounds them. At the very least, identifying the most important records will allow end-users to focus on them and reassure them that the rest of the information is not their concern. Ideally, of course, that redundant information, which may well include records, needs to be eliminated from the landscape as soon as possible.

Justifying records management

It is important to make the case for records management to ensure that there is both managerial support and adequate resource in place to support its successful implementation. We are going to look at what records management aims to achieve. We will also look at the broader context in which records management operates – the business environment. In justifying the implementation of a new records management programme, or overhaul of what is already in place, it is useful not only to enumerate the benefits, but also the risks of not doing so.

Aims of records management

As we have already seen, records management is about the control of records (and sometimes other information) to ensure reliability, facilitate access, comply with external obligations such as legislation and regulation, and to manage resources effectively. This overall goal of control breaks down into a number of more detailed aims, as follows:

- to design and set up secure systems, procedures and services to capture,

maintain, retrieve and dispose of the records necessary to provide reliable evidence of activities and decisions
- to achieve operational efficiency in record creation, access, retrieval and disposal so that it is fit for purpose, streamlined and efficient, and specifically so that records are:
  - comprehensively and reliably created or captured
  - easily and quickly found when needed
  - physically with or linked to other relevant records to provide the 'whole story'
  - appraised and tagged according to their retention value
  - destroyed according to retention schedules
- to control the volume and maintenance costs of records and eliminate the overheads associated with maintenance of obsolete records and informational material
- to support decision-making and business operations or activities by providing accurate records of what has happened in the past or current policy
- to provide evidence of policies, decisions and activities through records of what has occurred
- to meet legal and regulatory requirements, relevant standards and also professional and ethical responsibilities with respect to the creation and maintenance of certain records for specified periods of time
- to ensure that the records management programme itself has integrity through covering the entire lifecycle, including a timely destruction process, so as to demonstrate transparent and accountable business practices.

All of these aims need to be pursued across the organization and regardless of the format, the specific creator or the location of the records.

The wider context

Before we move on to risks and benefits, let's look at the wider context in which records management operates. It is important to understand the technological and general cultural environment in which business is conducted in order to explain how recordkeeping both depends upon it, but can also really improve its performance.

There are some crucial factors that records managers need to be aware of which influence record creation and use. The main ones are:

- legislation and the regulatory environment
- the increasing emphasis around the world in both the private and public

sectors on good governance, accountability and transparency
- computer and telecommunication technology and the changes they continue to bring to working practices, including the continuing development of technology to manage and control records
- the proliferation of recorded information and the increased dependence on it by business
- the increasingly vast array of options and solutions for digital storage
- the demise of dedicated filing staff and devolution of records management to the end-user
- the increasing pressure on individual employees due to the financial down-turn, heavier workloads, longer hours and the constant availability of work systems out of hours.

We can see from these relatively few factors that the environment is complex and challenging, but once we recognize them, we can begin to address them. Records management can have a positive impact on most of the issues these factors can raise. Table 3.2 shows how.

Table 3.2 *Addressing environmental factors*

Factor	Solution
1 Legislation and the regulatory environment	Being aware of the implications for records management in terms of requirements for retention, retrieval and destruction; ensuring the organization has adequate legal advice
2 The increasing emphasis on good governance, accountability and transparency	Ensuring good recordkeeping is in place to provide evidence and manage access rights
3 Computer and telecommunication technology and the changes they continue to bring to working practices, including the continuing development of technology to manage and control records	Advocating systems which create, manage and retain reliable records and which facilitate good recordkeeping practice
4 The proliferation of recorded information and business's increased dependence on it	Identifying and tagging information and records according to value and retention requirements; seeking efficient systems which do not increase administrative workloads
5 The increasingly vast array of options and solutions for digital storage	Tracking existing and specifying new records storage to ensure it is fit for purpose
6 The demise of dedicated filing staff and devolution of records management to the end-user	Providing appropriate, streamlined records management systems and training end-users in their operation
7 The increasing pressure on individual employees due to the financial downturn, heavier workloads, longer hours and the constant availability of work systems out of hours	Flagging the importance and relevance of records management to support business; seeking efficient systems which do not increase administrative workloads

The risks of poor records management

If an organization does not include the records management function in its corporate strategy it is likely to suffer accountability failures (either internal or external) because of its record systems. Without effective records management organizations are vulnerable if called upon to provide evidence of legal compliance, good governance or to defend their rights in court. For example, losing a court case or tribunal might result in fines and financial penalties (not to mention the cost of litigation in the first place) and there will also be an associated loss of reputation and trust. But the risks are not confined to such public exposure and failure. Lack of records management can lead to a waste of resources which are unnecessarily spent on physical and computer storage as well as staff time spent unproductively looking for, repeatedly moving around and unnecessarily copying and saving versions of identical information and records. If the most crucial records to support the running of the organization are not identified and protected, it will be unable to cope with and recover from a disaster. Without good records management organizations have no clear corporate memory and are doomed to continuously reinvent the wheel and repeat mistakes with all the waste of resources and lack of progress that entails. Finally, as we have already touched on in the section on information overload above, poor records management has an extremely debilitating effect on staff morale and stress levels.

The benefits of effective records management

There are many reasons to implement records management and to constantly review existing systems to ensure they are working effectively. Often the benefits are the reverse side of the risk coin – for example, good recordkeeping helps provide evidence of rights, decision-making and actions and thus can avoid fines and bad publicity. More generally, it ensures and demonstrates compliance with legislation, regulation and standards. It can save staff time and the cost of storage. Good recordkeeping often underpins all kinds of audit work, from financial to operational-specific. Records management also provides information security because records are identified and protected as an asset. Also, the archives are identified, protected and preserved in good order. All of these benefits contribute towards greater business efficiency, and the reduction of staff stress levels as they can be confident they are in control of the records.

Making the case

There is no ready-made case that will immediately convince management – and co-workers – that records management should be in place and invested in adequately. There are real-life examples of savings to be made in storage costs and some complex calculations demonstrating that quantifiable amounts of staff time can be saved through having recordkeeping systems in place that speed up filing and retrieval time. There are also examples of organizations which have suffered severe losses of reputation or financial assets due to an event – be it a court case or a disaster – which has been caused by their poor recordkeeping. However, it can be hard to find the ones that will strike a chord with any given organization. As a result building the case to justify records management needs to be carefully planned. There are initially two main stakeholders to convince: the management level that will authorize dedicated staff and equipment resources and the end-users whose time and knowledge of the records is needed to develop the system. The latter can be won over once management has endorsed the case, but before planning your records management programme, it is best to have management backing. How you build the case will depend on the overall corporate culture and what mixture of benefits, risks and factual evidence is likely to be most convincing in that organization. How you make the pitch – through a detailed report, a memorandum, a face-to-face meeting or a formal presentation – will again depend upon organizational culture.

Planning the records management programme

It is important to plan the records management programme carefully, including scoping the parameters of the project so that you can quantify the resources needed. Mostly this will be staff time – yours and end-users' – but it is also possible to do this kind of project on a consultancy basis, either commercially or by charging back to other departments or the business as a whole.

The plan needs to encompass five phases: scoping the programme; developing the policy and procedures; awareness-raising, training, dealing with legacy systems and records; and review. The various constituents can be broken down as follows:

- surveying
- drafting policies and procedures
- applying governance
- retention schedules
- non-current recordkeeping systems
- disposal
- vital records
- disaster planning
- implementation
- raising awareness
- legacy systems
- review.

These components (which will be familiar from the table of contents for this chapter) are not necessarily linear over time and the exact order in which they need to be tackled will depend on the organization and the particular recordkeeping environment.

Planning the records management programme requires you to understand your organization, its structure, goals, existing filing and computing practices and general attitude to records management. In particular, you will need to find out about the following:

- **Organizational structure:** to plan the survey you need a list of representative individuals from every work area, so at this stage the reason for looking at the organizational structure is to identify the groups and individuals which create and maintain discrete recordkeeping systems in order to map out the survey work. It may be a department, a team or a single member of staff which realizes the function and related activities. It won't be necessary to survey everyone in the organization, just representatives from each work area.
- **Existing recordkeeping systems:** the survey also needs to include information about existing recordkeeping systems and, whilst a lot of this information can be gathered during the survey, there may be documentation that provides useful background. Examples of this include policies mentioning records and use of IT, file lists and file plans, filing rules, shared drive structures (which can be rendered as screen shots), retention guidelines, procedures for putting records in non-current storage. Anything pertaining to the way individuals and teams manage or aspire to manage their records is useful. The project plan must allow time to review this material.
- **IT infrastructure:** since most modern records are created and held in digital format, the set-up of the organization's IT infrastructure is crucial to understanding the current records management situation and to finding ways to implement new solutions. It is important to include both consultation time with the IT colleagues responsible for the computer infrastructure and time to look at the systems to assess strengths and weaknesses from the records management perspective.
- **Particular impetus for records management at this point in time:** the specific reasons the organization has for overhauling or setting up the records management programme help to scope the project. Benchmarking the project methodology to meet that original need will ensure management and staff understand the reason for the records management programme and appreciate its goals. Moreover, the project aims have to reflect the original impetus, for example improving

performance or eliminating the risk associated with poor records management. This does not mean necessarily that other elements of the records management programme could be left out – just that the priorities will reflect the organization's identified needs and the original driver for records management.

This book includes all possible elements of a records management (RM) programme for paper and digital records but you will need to decide which parts you need to prioritize and emphasize. Some parts (for example vital records management) might be a lower priority and thus left to be implemented later on. Table 3.3 gives a list of all the different parts, together with guidance on how to estimate the time needed.

The exact amount of time required to establish a records management programme will very much depend on your own organization – the size, of course, but also how long it takes to get a major new initiative going and how ready it is for change. Once you have decided on the elements to include from the list of component parts, you will be in a position to work out what is needed and how long it will take to establish a records management programme.

Scoping the record survey

The aim of the record survey is to identify all areas of the organization and gather information about the records that the end-users create, receive and use. Using organizational charts and/or the knowledge of an experienced colleague, you should be able to make a list of all those areas and start to decide which individuals or teams you need to talk to. You will not need to speak to everyone, just the people who can speak for an organizational unit and know how the records are kept. With organizations where the work is divided on a geographic or other appropriate basis, it may be possible to interview a couple of sample teams and develop a blueprint that can be tailored to the other teams doing the same work. Examples of this kind of organizational structure might be a natural history museum where the departments each specialize in a specific area, such as entomology or mammals, or a local government social services department where teams of social workers are dedicated to different locations.

Let's take the example of the fictional Milson Widget Company (MWC), whose organizational chart is given in Figure 3.2.

We might expect to have 15 survey interviews with representatives from the various business teams as follows:

Table 3.3 *Component parts of the records management programme*

Part	How to assess time required
Senior management support	This entails getting their attention and making the case, either directly in person, or via a champion, such as your line manager.
Records management policy	It will not take long to look at a few examples, decide what to include and write the policy in keeping with your organization's documentation style.
Briefing for staff and management	This will require drafting some material – a leaflet and/or a PowerPoint and possibly scheduling and presenting the briefing to groups of staff.
Records survey	This depends on the size of your organization.
Retention schedules	It is hard to assess how long this will take as it depends on the number of record series as well as on the type of work and records of each particular organization – estimate about 30–50% (depending on your experience) of the time it took to survey the records, with time lag to allow for dialogue with record creators, users and other stakeholders.
Current filing improvement	You need time to analyse the existing system, identify improvements, document your findings, advise the individual or team and support them in implementing the improvements.
Retention schedule training for end-users	This entails developing some guidelines and either talking through them on a case-by-case basis or providing more general training sessions.
Set-up and ongoing maintenance and control of physical non-current record storage	See below for all of the elements involved in setting up non-current storage for physical records. Allow time to create database, to label and log physical locations and map to them the details of records as they come into storage, establish procedures for retrieving and returning material and for regularly reviewing, destroying and documenting material as it becomes due.
Set-up and ongoing maintenance and control of digital record storage	Setting up digital storage is dependent on access to and liaison with good IT expertise, as well as establishing the system for logging records with metadata as they come in, a system for auditing and recording access and procedures and documentation for deleting material according to retention rules.
Vital records identification and protection	This entails surveying and agreeing the vital records and deciding and establishing protection methods, recall or destruction/deletion of copies when records are no longer vital, and training staff in operating the system and emergency recovery.
Documenting the RM system	Most of the documentation will be created as you establish the programme but you should allow some time to pull it all together and fill in any gaps.
Records management awareness-raising and establishing a good recordkeeping culture	Establishing a good recordkeeping culture comes out of the work in establishing the programme, but allocate some time during this stage, as well as afterwards, to finding ways to keep records management in the minds of all staff.
Initial induction and refresher training for end-users	This requires planning, drafting of handout materials for trainees and scheduling and delivering training.
Training and continuing professional development for RM staff	This should be part of every organization's human resources policy, but the records manager plans and identifies relevant training for themselves and for staff in the team.
Records management audit	A records management audit can take almost as long as the initial records survey, analysis and report takes.
Overall records management programme review	This could be done in 3–5 days, provided there was audit data available, depending on the size and scope of the records management programme and how detailed it needs to be.

1 The Executive Assistant to the Head of Development (1 person)
2 The Development Department's design team (3 people)
3 The Head of Production (1 person)
4 One Lead Production Technician and a Production Technician (2 people)
5 Head of Marketing and Sales (1 person)
6 One Sales Representative and an Assistant (2 people)
7 Milson Widgets Shop Manager and a Sales Assistant (2 people)
8 The Personal Assistant to the Executive Director/Head of Product Support (1 person)
9 The Head of Facilities and the Facilities Assistant (2 people)
10 The HR team (3 people)
11 The Head of Finance (1 person)
12 The Bookkeepers (2 people)
13 The Accountants (2 people)
14 The Payroll Clerk (1 person)
15 The Shipping Clerk (1 person).

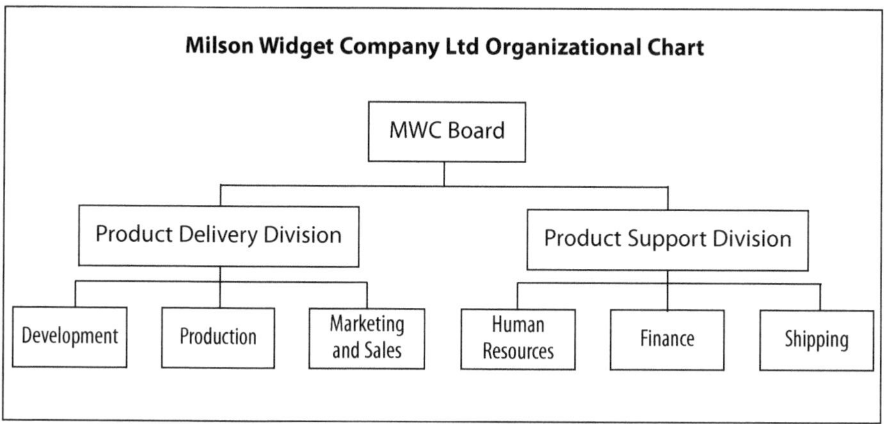

Figure 3.2 *Milson Widget Company Ltd organizational chart*

Thus, in terms of the record survey itself, we know we should talk to 15 teams (no more than 25 people), and should schedule 15 interviews. We also know that most MWC staff are based at the factory in the East End of London, but the shop is in Baker Street (Central London), so travel time to the shop may need to be factored into the interview schedule. Record survey interviews generally take about an hour, but it is best to allocate an hour and a half in case more time is needed. It is not sensible to conduct more than three interviews a day, because the process requires a lot of concentration on the part of the interviewer.

We also need to gather information about the IT platform in order to begin to see how recordkeeping works in the organization. In the case of MWC, IT support is outsourced and the Facilities Manager is the person who manages the contract – so additional time with the Facilities Manager is needed and it would be very useful to speak to the person in the IT company who leads on the MWC contract.

To schedule record survey interviews plus the IT special interview, with a maximum of three interviews per day, you would need six or seven working days. However, it may well not be possible to schedule all the interviews consecutively. You also need to allow time to develop material to notify management and staff that the survey will be happening and give some background on the overall records management implementation plan and its aims. The earlier sections on benefits and risks and on briefings opposite will help you to develop this material.

Once the interviews are completed you will need to write them up, analyse the findings and develop retention schedules as well as develop a records management programme that meets the needs of the organization. This will probably take the same amount of time again as you have spent on the interview process. Figure 3.3 illustrates the overall times that might be needed in our MWC project.

Task/step	Time	Notes
Development of forms and briefing materials, setting up database	2 days	
Scheduling interviews	2 days	Cannot complete schedule all at once, need to allow people to return calls or e-mail, etc.
Management briefing	1 hour	
Interviews	7 days	May not be able to do in consecutive days, depending on people's availability
Writing up and analysis, development of retention schedules	7 days	May need to refer back to interviewees, so may not be able to do in consecutive days
Drafting records management policy and procedures	2 days	
Approval of RM policy	1 hour	Presentation at Board
Scheduling follow-up meetings	1 day	
Review and agreement of retention schedules, training in implementing schedules	6 days	May not be able to do in consecutive days
Scheduling workshops	1 day	
Paper and digital records workshops	8 days	May not be able to do in consecutive days
Scheduling recordkeeping follow-up meetings	1 day	
Review of paper and digital recordkeeping progress	8 days	May not be able to do in consecutive days
Audit of records management programme	14 days	Do at least one year after programme implementation and no more than 18 months after. May not be able to do in consecutive days, allow for scheduling meeting times, staff availability, writing up and reporting back to Board and teams as appropriate.

Figure 3.3 *Scoping MWC Ltd's records management implementation project*

Preparation

Before you can start the records survey, you need to draft some forms to capture all the survey data you need in a consistent manner. You also need to brief the people you are interviewing – and their managers – about the aims and intended outcomes of the survey and the project as a whole. Finally, you will need to schedule the interviews.

Briefings

Briefings can be delivered as formal presentations, informal meetings or as e-mail memos or leaflets; the most effective way of doing it will depend on organizational culture.

Management briefings need to focus on a few high-level points, including:

- benefits of good records management
- risks of not having records management
- staff time and involvement required
- management commitment to the records management project: encouragement of staff to engage with the survey and resulting records management systems; taking measures if staff do not comply with the project requirements.

Staff briefings should also include the goals, benefits and risks, but they also need to be more detailed, covering:

- the time the interview will take (usually about an hour)
- the kind of questions that will be asked – mostly easy to answer about the work done and the records that are created and used
- reassurance that the point of the interviews is to benchmark, not to find fault or judge.

Forms and data collection

Interviews will centre on a set of questions designed to find out what staff do, the importance of what they do, what records they use and create, how long the records are needed and what their existing records management practices are like. The data needs to be collected such that it can be combined and sorted in various ways. Word tables, spreadsheets and databases can be used very effectively for this purpose – obviously it is a good idea to set up the forms so that they feed easily into the cumulative document and it is important to bear in mind the information needed to develop retention schedules. The sections that follow cover interviewing and retention schedule development and discuss the documentation needed.

Scheduling Interviews

Organizing the interviews can be surprisingly time-consuming. It is important, as already noted, to identify the right people to speak to. Getting people to focus on the need to meet and to commit to a time can require a lot of patience and perseverance. Remember that conducting the interviews requires considerable concentration, so it is best to allow at least a half-hour between interviews and to have no more than three in one day. The schedule must be managed for the duration of the survey as people may need to rearrange appointments.

Surveying

As already mentioned, the main point of the record survey is to identify and evaluate records created and used by the organization in order to manage them efficiently in accordance with legal, business and societal requirements. The outcome will be all or most aspects of a records management programme, such as policy, procedures, retention schedules, vital records protection plans, etc. The record survey should also reveal levels of duplication both within and across media and permit identification of the master copy and its medium.

It is possible to conduct the survey without interviewing, if you send the questionnaires out and request staff to complete the form themselves, or create an online survey. However, the best way to do it is by interview, because it prevents misunderstandings about the questions (and the nature and importance of the records) and it also provides the records manager with a very important first contact for building awareness of the importance of records management and buy-in to the programme. You can send the questionnaire out before the interview so that staff are prepared for the questions – but make it clear that you will be filling it out together during the meeting.

The questionnaire

The questions asked during the survey interview are key to getting the right information to ensure the records management programme is designed well and fit for purpose. Checklist 3.1 provides a list of data for inclusion in the survey interview.

Checklist 3.1 Survey data

Identification data

- Reference, unique to the interview

- Date of interview
- Interviewer
- Interviewee

Organization data

- Interviewee's job title
- Interviewee's department/section/team
- What do you do? What are the individual/team responsibilities, activities, functions? What is the work cycle and deadlines?
- Which other teams or individuals share your records?

General recordkeeping data

- Who does the paper filing?
- Is there a centralized paper filing system?
- Are there any non-current records in off-site storage?
- Is there a file plan or file classification scheme? (request copies)
- Is there a shared team drive? (request screen shots)
- What sort of records are kept on personal drives? (request screen shots)
- Is there a system for version control? (describe)
- How is personal e-mail organized?
- Is there a system for sharing and saving e-mails all the team need to see? (describe)

Record data

- Record series name
- Medium
- Who creates the records?
- Who uses the records?
- Are the records masters or copies?
- Is the record series archival?
- Overall retention period before destruction/deletion
- When can the records be transferred to non-current storage?
- Reason for the retention decision including any legislation which affects retention of the records

Vital records

- Is it a vital record?
- How is the record protected?
- When do the records cease to be vital?
- Recovery/reconstitution plan

Security

- Are there security/privacy/commercial confidentiality issues?
- Are there particular access permissions for the series?

General

- Are there any particular concerns about managing records?

Conducting the interviews

Before embarking on an interview make sure you have a copy of the form, with extra copies of the page for collecting the record series information and extra paper for notes, as well as a spare pen or pencil.

Start the interview by confirming that the interviewee knows what the project is about – even if they have read or attended the briefing, they usually welcome a short update. Reassure them that you are not inspecting or auditing but rather identifying good practice and to help them find good ways of managing their records. The main task is to draw out the interviewee to gather the necessary data. But remember this is also a golden opportunity to raise awareness and get people to realize that the records manager can help and provide advice and support – give tips and recommendations at the interview stage if you can.

Most of the data should be fairly straightforward to collect, people know what they do and the records they use and enjoy talking about it. Identifying the record series is perhaps the most difficult, as most people will not think of records in this way. Use open questions like 'tell me about what you do' and 'what kinds of records do you keep?' to get people to think about their work and records. As you help them to identify groups of records as series, they will begin to understand what is required. Remember that for many people, there is no clear distinction between records and information, or the records which come from outside sources and are therefore not records of their own organization. It may be necessary to note down information series like the collection of annual reports from competing businesses held by the Executive Director's PA or the stationery catalogues used by the Head of Procurement in order to clearly assign it a 'retain as long as of current business use' value in the retention schedule. It can also be hard to find out – and understand – where the computer records are saved. It takes a little while to learn how to conduct a survey interview, but even experienced interviewers sometimes need to ask interviewees later for clarification or additional information.

Finish the interview by explaining what the next steps are, let the interviewee know when to expect a draft retention schedule for comment and outline other aspects of the programme such as policy and procedures.

One further tip: it can be very effective to conduct the interviews in pairs, particularly if you are new to the process.

Writing up

After the interviews the data needs to be rationalized and analysed. The precise nature of the resulting written documentation will depend on the particular aims and shape of the organizational records management programme but the outputs might include:

- an overall report on recordkeeping in the organization
- individual reports for each team on its recordkeeping with recommendations for improvement
- paper record classification schemes and/or file structures for digital records
- reports and recommendations on aspects of recordkeeping such as vital records, confidentiality, security
- retention schedules.

It is best to process the interview data as soon as possible after the interviews but it will also be necessary to wait until all the interviews have been conducted to get the full picture in order to develop consistent and comprehensive retention schedules, policies and procedures. Retention schedules and reports relating to individuals' and teams' recordkeeping systems need to be returned in draft form to them for any changes and confirmation of details.

Digital records issues

If the goals of the records management programme include improving and rationalizing digital recordkeeping practice across the organization, the survey needs to gather detailed information about the organization's IT set-up and the way teams and individuals organize and use the records and the available technology.

Technical issues

You need to have one or more technical meetings with IT staff at the relevant level to develop an understanding of how the IT platform works, identify the various systems which create records and the server space, together with access protocols. This will help you to make recommendations and draft procedures for managing digital records in the current IT system, as well as specify and implement improved IT systems to support more effective records management. There is a very close relationship between software and document format, the IT skills and knowledge of the users, their records management awareness and the ability of an organization to be good at managing its records. Thus records management can help end-users learn how computer functionality can support and streamline their work. For example, the IT system allows authorized (and proficient) end-users to download images from recognized digital cameras into designated drives and the end-users also know how to rename a batch of digital images (previously having automatically generated numbers as names) in one operation to provide the whole set of images with the same meaningful name plus a running number.

Digital records management

The best way to investigate current digital recordkeeping practices is to have meetings with groups of staff using the same shared areas of IT network space. Because modern computer technology tends to encourage idiosyncratic and individual filing habits and behaviour within shared recordkeeping systems, it is important to get everyone sharing the drive around the table to discuss the existing system and identify the strengths and weaknesses in current ways of working.

This calls for an approach which is part interview and part workshop and will probably need more than one meeting. Essentially the records manager is acting as facilitator, data gatherer and consultant all at once. It takes experience, a mix of records management and interpersonal skills and confidence and is best done by two records management staff working together. This means one person can lead in asking questions and facilitating discussion and decision-making, and the other can take notes and act as a prompter. It works well as an additional phase of the records management project, following on after the survey and initial implementation of the retention schedules and other RM procedures. This allows any changes to current structures and practices to take into account and support the retention requirements; for example, having annual folders makes it easy to delete them all at once when the retention period is over.

Workshops like this can take as long as two hours. There can be resistance to having the whole team out of the office at one time but once the workshop gets going people often appreciate the chance to take time out as a group and look at the way they use and manage their records and to reflect on the way they work. Effective group decisions can be made about the big things – such as how to organize the folder structure or what to do about legacy records which have languished since the ex-staff member left. Some action can be taken, for example deleting obviously redundant or duplicate records or combining or splitting folders in line with the group's emerging classification principles. Generally team members leave the meeting having committed to tasks which will complete the reorganization and improvement of digital recordkeeping systems. The records managers provide a report on the team's records management status prior to the workshop, actions and decisions taken in the workshop and an action plan for further work, together with any draft procedures that may have emerged. Checklist 3.2 outlines the process for carrying out digital records workshops.

Checklist 3.2 The process for digital records workshops

Logistics

- Identification of team members and invitation to attend workshop
- Large room, preferably with a boardroom style layout so that everyone can sit around the table and see the screen
- A computer terminal linked to the network, in particular the shared areas of the team in question
- List of issues and questions to cover, space to note the folder structure
- Statistics on server space taken up by team documents and number of folders and documents, at start of workshop.

Workshop activity

- Identification of drives used by team, discussion of how used, assessment of structures and naming conventions
- Identification of non-standard systems (e.g. HR, Finance), discussion of what used for, technical issues, where records reside and how managed
- Mapping of data flows within and in and out of team
- Identification – and resolution of – duplication, file and folder naming issues, classification principles
- Immediate action where possible (e.g. deleting records, re-foldering)
- Start to map out better structures and procedures.

Post-workshop documentation

- Report giving:
  — summary of existing digital recordkeeping practice
  — details of actions taken during the workshop
  — details of decisions made regarding organization, naming conventions, etc.
  — action plan for future work
- Interim and final statistics on server space taken up by team documents and number of folders and documents.

Table 3.4 suggests the various spaces the workshops need to address, the information needed and what the end-result should be. Table 3.5 gives an

Table 3.4 *Issues to cover in digital records workshop*

Space	What information needed	With view to providing
Shared drive	Name and description of how currently organized	Optimal folder structure as agreed by team; guidelines and procedures; responsibilities for team members for use, monitoring and deletion according to retention requirements
Other drives	Names, how organized, what used for	Overall guidance on what to use for; specific folder structures, guidelines, procedures and responsibilities
Non-standard systems (e.g. financial, HR)	What used for, how maintained, training provided, where records reside, how they are deleted	Assessment of reliability, accessibility and security of records; recommendations for improvement; retention requirements and procedures
E-mail	How organized, how shared within team, retention practice	Guidelines for use, organization, sharing, retention formats and deletion
Images	How created, saved, organized, named, shared	Guidelines on formats and resolution, naming, organizing, sharing, retention, metadata requirements
Cloud solutions	What is used, where records reside, security issues, technical issues	Guidelines on what to use for, security measures, contract provision and conditions with providers

Table 3.5 *Example of documentation of folder structures and improvement plan for shared drive*

Path and end folder name	What used for, how documents named	Actions	Notes
Shared/5 projects	Records of all projects managed by the team	Older folders need reviewing to identify records past retention dates and to ensure organized and records named according to agreed filing procedures. Senior Project Manager to ensure all team members comply.	
Shared/5 projects/ organizational projects	All projects run in-house, organized by folder named by project title	Going forward project folders to be named with project ref (YYYY-running number-abbreviated name)	Consider renaming old projects, also setting up folders for completed projects according to retention expiry date for ease of deletion
Shared/5 projects/funded projects	All funded project documentation, organized by folder with project ref as name (YYYY-running number-abbreviated name)	Ensure older project documentation folders comply – Senior Project Manager responsible	Consider setting up folders for completed projects according to retention expiry date for ease of deletion
Shared/5 projects/funded projects/2013-001-pavement-art	All records for pavement art project, numbered and named according to project record filing procedures	None	Well organized, documented procedures

example of how to document folder structures (in this case the shared drive) and decisions on how to improve records management within them.

E-mail management

The records survey cannot ignore the issue of e-mail, since it is such a common tool in contemporary business life and all organizations use it. There is no one simple solution to managing e-mail records effectively but the survey and the resulting records management procedures have to address the following aspects of e-mail management:

- making sure that end-users can recognize when e-mail, and/or any attachments, are records
- organizing e-mail to support end-users' work
- saving or moving e-mail to areas with related records in other formats where they can be accessed by all the people who are authorized and have the need
- ensuring redundant e-mail is deleted
- ways to deal with information overload issues associated with e-mail.

The technical discussions with IT staff should help you to understand what the IT platform currently supports, as well as possibilities for future development of the IT infrastructure to support better integration of e-mail that are records into the records management system.

Systems for digital records management

One potential way to manage all digital records, regardless of format, in one automated system is to use electronic records management software. However, successful scope and implementation is a difficult and resource-intensive proposition, quite apart from the expense of the software itself. Total digital records management cannot be achieved without records management processes and documentation, as described in this section. It also usually requires a lot of work on the additional and time-consuming tasks of developing an organization-wide classification scheme and metadata schema. For this reason Electronic Records Management Systems (ERMS) are usually only successful when implemented by large organizations. It is not possible to go into detail about how to implement ERMS here, but general records management principles and techniques as outlined in this chapter provide the necessary basis, combined with the ability to communicate effectively with IT colleagues. Checklist 3.3 summarizes the main steps for implementing ERMS.

Checklist 3.3 Implementing electronic records management systems

1 Survey the organization's digital records and the way they are currently managed.
2 Analyse the record survey data to:
   - estimate the number of digital records to be included and the growth rate
   - identify the various document formats that need to be included
   - identify issues around corporate culture and change management, for example attitudes to sharing documents and drives, perceived ownership, duplication habits.
3 List the existing procedures and documentation for records management and:
   - identify the gaps
   - make any adjustments.
4 Start to work on filling the gaps, for example developing the classification scheme, or retention schedules.
5 Talk to your IT colleagues (this is sometimes the first step, particularly if the impetus for ERMS comes from the IT department).
6 Draft the functional specifications, using the standards for specifying ERMS and consulting with end-users and IT professionals.
7 Send the tender documentation, including the functional specification, out to potential vendors.
8 Review the tenders carefully against the functional specification, consult other records managers using the systems and make the decision based on how closely the vendors can match your requirements.
9 Once the software has been selected, make sure the records management team is represented in the project plan for implementation; for example, it should be leading on:
   - developing the classification scheme
   - developing the metadata schema, which will outline the set of information needed to tag documents for links, context and relationships, authentication and retention
   - specifying preferences and profiles for documents and actions on documents
   - training for different levels of users on the records management issues.
10 Get trained yourself.
11 Review ERMS and recordkeeping practices six months after implementation is complete.

Policy and procedures, implementation guidance

The records management policy and procedures provide the authority for and way of operating the records management programme. New programmes need implementation guidance that should evolve into operating procedures. Whilst all of this documentation can be drafted before the record survey work has been done, the documentation has to reflect the survey findings and the organizational culture. The policy and procedures also need to be consistent with, and refer to, related organizational policy.

Records management policy

The records management policy is the corner-stone of the records management programme. It is a clear message that the organization takes records management seriously, and, in organizations where access to information and information governance are obligatory, it underpins compliance with regulation and legislation.

The policy needs to include:

- a clear statement that the organization is committed to records management and is willing to provide the resources necessary to do so effectively
- identification of post-holders responsible for the various aspects of records management, for example the board member who acts as champion, the records manager who is responsible for all aspects of managing the records management programme and end-users who are responsible for carrying out specific tasks according to the policy and procedures
- the scope of the records management programme, which will define records and spell out that the policy covers all organizational records in all media
- the regulation and legislation which affects records management and to which the organization is subject
- the date of the policy, the review date and authorization by the organization's main governing body.

Implementation guidance

The records management team provides the most valuable support for staff implementing new records management procedures. They can ensure that end-users understand and are happy with what they need to do and, if necessary, help them to get started on some of the work. However, staff will also need implementation guidance and support. Table 3.6 gives a list of the sort of guidance that is useful for end-users.

Table 3.6 *Records management implementation guidance*

Type of guidance	Includes
Implementing retention schedules	• establishing a routine each year at a convenient time in the work cycle for closing files, listing non-current files and deleting or destroying records which meet retention periods • how to document destruction and deletion • what to do with archive records
Action plans for setting up or improving filing systems	• principles for organizing records into files and folders • a step-plan to review and reorganize records • how to document destruction and deletion • what to do with archive records • documenting the system
Guidance on developing naming conventions for records in shared drives and/or across organizations	• consulting with affected staff • options to consider • drafting document outlining the rules
Review of legacy records and archives	• step-plan to review legacy records • identifying and documenting archives • identifying and destroying redundant records • identifying and saving records required for ongoing business in line with records management system requirements

The table shows that the implementation guidance overlaps with procedures, for example 'Implementing retention schedules', 'Action plans for improving filing systems' and 'Review of legacy records' all refer to destruction and deletion, which (as outlined below) will have specific procedures.

Records management procedures

Any job of work that needs to be done repeatedly and continuously by more than one person needs to have written procedures to ensure it is done consistently over time by the different people with varying responsibilities for that work. Table 3.7 gives a list of procedures with notes on what they should include and cross-references to related records management implementation guidance and other relevant records management or organizational policy and procedures.

This book covers the principles of all of these aspects of managing records, and procedures can be drafted on this basis. As mentioned above, because the RM procedures need to be tailored to the organization, it is best to draft them after the record survey, ensuring that they work smoothly with and in the context of the overall work and working practices of the organization.

The role of legislation, regulation and standards

Before you can process the data gathered during the survey properly, you

Table 3.7 *Records management procedures*

Procedure	Content	Cross-reference
Using retention schedules	Establishing regular routine; closing files; documenting destruction and deletion; what to do with archive records.	Can be based on the retention schedule implementation guidance.
Operating current filing systems	How to file; how to open and document new files; following version control and naming convention rules; how to check out and return files.	Should be consistent with action plans for setting up or improving filing systems.
Naming conventions for documents, files and folders	Naming convention policy outlining rules for naming documents, files and folders.	Will be the result of following the guidance on developing naming conventions for records in shared drives and/or across organizations.
Version control guidelines	Details of the recommended system and how to follow it.	
Management of e-mail	How to manage e-mail effectively to reduce information overload; how to save e-mail with related records so everyone can access; identifying non-record e-mail and deleting it regularly.	Should refer to the IT e-mail policy.
Transferring records to non-current storage	Boxing up non-current records; listing and logging into the location system; adding retention date; how to retrieve non-current records if needed.	In accordance with retention schedules.
Record destruction	Documenting destruction; permissible methods of destruction.	In accordance with retention schedules.
Transferring records to the archives	Identifying archival records; handling and packaging them; documenting archival records.	Need to use the retention schedules.
Managing vital records	Identifying vital records; copying and/or sending to secure storage; removing out of date vital records; what to do in event of emergency.	Needs to map to the disaster prevention and recovery plan.

need to make sure that you understand the legal, regulatory and standards environment in which the organization works. It is not possible for a book like this one to give chapter and verse as to which laws, regulation and standards organizations need to comply with, because it is not a case of one size fits all. We will try to cover the main legislative areas that records managers need to be aware of, as well as regulatory issues and standards.

Archives and records management law

In many countries the first place to look for legal requirements for managing records is the law pertaining to the management of government records and archives. Whilst such legislation will impact predominantly on public bodies, it also provides national archives with a remit to provide guidance on standards and practices for the archives and records management sector as a whole. The nature and extent of this kind of legislation varies from country to country and can be difficult to understand. Here are some questions to ask to help you understand the terms and implications of such legislation:

Does this legislation affect my organization? Archive and records management legislation can be quite limited in its jurisdiction, just impacting on the records of central government. It can be more wide-ranging however, and relate to local government bodies such as city or county authorities. It is even possible that it might have implications for any body receiving public funding. Look for details of bodies covered by the law and for mention of a body (such as the national archives) with responsibility for ensuring that the law is adhered to, or for providing help to other bodies. Read the legislation and decide whether it is something your organization is obliged to comply with. List the specific legal requirements so that you can work through them and ensure you are – or will be – compliant.

What does this legislation say about records management? Archives legislation does not often explicitly state the need for records management to ensure that archives are identified and managed well. If the term 'records management' is not used, look for any reference to filing, classification, selection or destruction. Look also for reference to media – does it cover electronic or audiovisual records, for example? Identify the specific records management provisions and ensure that you have a checklist to use as the basis for action or audit. An audit will ensure the existing records management system – or the new one you are establishing – has everything in place to follow the law.

Which external organizations can provide me with help and information? Archives and records management legislation often gives government or national archives a role in supporting implementation of the legal provisions. Check whether the legislation mentions such a provision. Check the advisory/supervisory body's website for advice and guidance.

Are there any codes of practice or guidelines that relate to the law which we need to follow? If the law gives a body such as the national archives an advisory or supervisory role, see if it also refers to specific documentation or activity. Gather – and read – any codes of practice or guidance that has been developed under the legislation.

What does it say about archives – what do we have to do about our archival records? If you have got this far in your analysis, it is possible your organization's archival records will need to be deposited in the national archives. Look for reference to required deposit in a central repository, and whether there are any conditions whereby your organization could retain its archives. Decide whether depositing your archives is a good option for the organization. If it is not, start to list and implement the provisions for retaining your archival records.

Access to information legislation

Access to information legislation, also known as 'freedom of information' (abbreviated to FoI in the UK and FOIA in the USA), gives citizens the right to see information created by or used by government. Although rarely mentioning the word 'record' in the title of the law, such legislation is also about records and their management. As we have seen, information and records are often misunderstood by creators and users, but records are essentially a sub-set of the much larger information pool. Whilst many citizens looking for access to government information may not know it, they are usually looking for a record of what has occurred, what has been decided or what has been planned, how and why. The reliable evidence of this will be in the record, even if other information sources mention it. Access to information legislation is often part of a suite of legislation together with open data and open government legislation which may be combined or separate laws. Table 3.8 gives a comparative list of UK and US FoI legislation provision.

Table 3.8 *Comparison of UK and US Freedom of Information legislation*

UK Freedom of Information Act 2000	US Freedom of Information Act in 1966 (amended often since then)
Grants access rights to recorded information held by a wide range of bodies across the public sector, including local government and universities.	Provides the right to obtain access to federal agency records. It only applies to Executive Branch agencies of US central government.
Applies to information which is made available to the public on a routine basis as well as that which is not but must potentially be so if requested.	Applies to two categories of agency information (defined in the Act) that must 'automatically' be disclosed by federal agencies as well as records not made routinely available.
The public must be told whether the information exists and be granted access to it within 20 working days of the request.	Agencies have 20 working days to respond to the request.
Under the 2000 Act the Lord Chancellor was obliged to publish a records management code of practice to support government bodies (drafted and supported by The National Archives).	President Obama, in his Presidential Memorandum on Managing Government Records of November 2011, stated that 'proper records management is the backbone of open government'.
There are 24 exemptions, including exemptions which refer to other information legislation. 'Defence' and 'Commercial interest' are among them. According to the Act, if an exemption is to be claimed, it must have been subjected to the 'public interest' test to determine whether disclosure would be more in the public interest, than exempting it.	There are 9 exemptions, examples including 'Trade secrets' and 'National defence'. There is no public interest test with respect to determine exemption status, however Obama stated in his 2009 FOIA Memorandum that agencies should administer the Act 'with a clear presumption: in the face of doubt, openness prevails'.
The Information Commissioner is the ombudsman for regulating compliance with information legislation, including the Data Protection Act.	The Office of Government Information Services (part of the NARA, the US national archives) is the regulating body for the FOIA.

We have seen that the goals of records management include facilitating access to records, as well as ensuring that records no longer needed are destroyed promptly and the destruction authorization properly documented. There is therefore a clear relationship between the ability of public bodies to find and provide access to information and records and the way they manage those records. This is seen, perhaps not so clearly, in both the UK and the US approaches to providing legal rights to access government information and records. It is important to note that under the UK legislation it is an offence to alter or destroy records which have been requested under FoI. This does not mean that it is an offence to destroy records that are not subject to an ongoing request if appropriate retention schedules are in place as part of the records management programme.

If an organization is subject to FoI legislation, having a records management programme in place, regardless of whether the law specifically requires it, will make compliance easier and more resource effective.

Privacy legislation

Privacy legislation, or data protection, as the British call it, also affects management. Unlike archives legislation and access to government information, though, it will probably impact most organizations. Such legislation defines and governs the way personal information about individuals is gathered, managed, shared and destroyed – and is the reason you should include a question about personal data and records in the record survey. There are a few steps to follow to ensure the records management programme is set up to be in compliance with the prevailing privacy legislation in your country:

1 Ensure you understand what information is 'personal' and if there are categories of personal data that the law defines as especially sensitive.
2 Identify all the personal information and records captured and held in the organization: the human resources department is a good place to start but many parts of the organization will manage staff or maintain contact lists; the survey will help you to identify everything.
3 Work out what records management and security processes need to be in place to ensure compliance with the law: restrict access to paper and digital records containing personal data; institute rigorous destruction processes for personal records to ensure that they are not kept longer than needed or is lawful; make sure that lawful access can be given promptly to individuals who are the subject of the data; find a way to give access to others without breaching the law, for example by blocking out (or redacting) names and other identifying elements in the records.

In the UK the Data Protection Act of 1998 specifies that personal information that is out of date and/or no longer required for the purpose for which it was collected may not be kept. However, this is a potential problem for archival records, because many records containing personal data have always been destined for and kept in archives. For this reason the UK law has an exemption to allow personal data to be retained for research, history and statistics purposes.

Statutes of limitation

Another useful aspect of the law to be aware of when mapping your records management environment is legislation which sets a time limit for prosecution. In the UK this is generally six years, but US federal law only specifies five. There are exceptions for both countries, so it is important to check out the law properly and to be sure that record retention schedules reflect the need to keep records providing evidence that might be required in court for the requisite amount of time. This especially goes for areas that may be susceptible to litigation.

Financial and tax legislation

Financial and tax legislation will have an important impact on records management, particularly retention. Accounting and financial professionals usually have a good understanding of (and measures in place to comply with) provisions respecting how long to retain records before they can be destroyed or deleted.

Apart from the general framework of tax and financial legislation, in the last decade or so, additional legislation has been enacted in a number of countries which specifically addresses corporate governance practices and the records that underpin transparency. In the USA, the Sarbanes–Oxley Act of 2002 was passed as a direct result of a number of scandals, most notably the Enron/Anderson case of 2001, arising from fiscal reporting failure and impropriety in the financial sector. The 'SOX' Act has a significant impact on records management not only on US companies but also any operating in the USA:

- requiring CEOs and Chief Financial Officers to personally certify that periodic financial disclosures filed with the US Securities and Exchange Commission (SEC) accurately reflect the company's financial condition
- mandating retention requirements for certain types of records
- criminalizing executives or employees tampering with or destroying accounting records and the destruction or mutilation of corporate records with the intention of impeding or influencing a government investigation.

Similar legislation was enacted in a number of other countries, but in the UK the emerging need for stricter financial governance was countered with a regulatory Corporate Governance Code overseen by the Financial Reporting Council, the independent regulator for corporate governance and reporting.

Other legislation

It is rare for the text of laws to refer clearly and specifically to records and to provide a clear indication of what records should be made and kept and for how long. However, records are the best way to demonstrate compliance with the law. The record survey should have revealed areas where legal requirements play an important role in the work of colleagues. Depending on the kind of organization, you should also check out some or all of the following:

- health and safety legislation and related regulations
- legislation affecting the operation of legal companies and corporations
- charities legislation.

This book is not intended to give detailed legal guidance, but rather to provide the tools for identifying and finding out more about dealing with the legal issues that people managing records and archives need to be aware of and with which the organization needs to comply. It is important to do some research into the legislation, look at any relevant professional guidance and to take legal advice if you are able to.

The regulatory environment

You will also need to take into account the regulatory environment in which your organization operates. There are two main aspects to the regulatory environment: generally applicable regulation associated with law – for example, in the UK, health and safety requirements have the force of law because they are required by 'headline legislation' – and regulation mandated by the watchdog of specific industries, such as the pharmaceutical industry. Other regulated industries include the food industry (in some countries regulated jointly with the pharmaceutical industry, energy supply industries, financial services and/or investment (as we saw already in the section on financial legislation) and real estate. In general regulators require compliance with regulations and the best way of demonstrating compliance is by good recordkeeping, but some regulation is very specific about recordkeeping responsibilities. The good news is that regulators generally produce a lot of guidance and advice on how to comply with the regulation.

Standards

> **Standard:** 'A thing, quality or specification by which something may be tested or measured; an established or accepted model; a definite level of excellence or adequacy required, aimed at, or possible.'[1]

The recordkeeping field has a range of standards which you need to know about and should aspire to meet. We cannot cover them all here, but we will discuss some of the most useful ones.

International standards

There are a number of standards created or endorsed by the International Organization for Standardization (ISO). The page listing the standards and projects under the direct responsibility of the Archives/records management Secretariat (ISO/TC 46/SC 11)[2] is a good place to start.

The International Records Management Standard, **ISO 15489:2001**: *Information and documentation – records management,* arguably the most significant standard for us, consists of two parts, a general overview and the detailed specification. The latter gives a detailed list of all the things that need to be in place to have a records management programme of an internationally recognized standard. It provides the best list of all the elements that need to be in place for a good records management programme.

ISO 23081: *Information and documentation – managing metadata for records* is a standard for creating and managing recordkeeping metadata. It consists of three parts:

- principles
- conceptual and implementation issues
- self-assessment method.

ISO/TR 18128:2014: *Information and documentation – risk assessment for records processes and systems* is a technical report with guidance and examples for assessing risks to records processes and systems in compliance with ISO 31000, the risk management standard.

ISO/TR 17068:2012: *Information and documentation – trusted third party repository for digital records* details the authorized custody services of a Trusted Third Party Repository (TTPR) in order to ensure provable integrity and authenticity of the clients' digital records and serve as a source of reliable evidence.

Standards for digital records management systems

For the past 20 years or so, there has been an awareness amongst archivists and records managers, as well as responsible organizations wishing to take advantage of developments in technology, that the systems in which records are created and maintained play a key role in ensuring that the records are reliable and accessible for as long as they need to be, that they can be organized in ways to reflect their interrelationships and to support work processes. There are three main standards, as follows.

ISO 16175: *Principles and functional requirements for records in electronic office environments*, in three parts including an overview, a specification for dedicated digital records management and one for general business systems, was published in 2010/2011. It is based on the standard of the same name developed by the International Council on Archives between 2006 and 2008, more informally called ICA-Req. The standard provides a set of functional requirements that must be in place for the system to be compliant and to be considered a recordkeeping system. ICA has developed a range of supporting material including implementation guides, advocacy literature and training modules. You can use the standard to audit existing systems or procure new ones.

Modular Requirements for Records Systems (MoReq) is a *de facto* standard – not ratified by a standards authority as such, but based on work commissioned and reviewed by experts in the field. It emanates from the DLM Forum, a multidisciplinary group set up by the European Commission in 1994 with the goal of investigating, promoting and implementing possibilities for wider co-operation in the field of electronic archives among and for its members. There have been three editions and the current one is MoReq2010.

Department of Defense Directive 5015.02-STD: the US Department of Defense realized early on the benefits of having a standard for all parts of its large organization to adhere to and to require vendors to follow. The *Electronic Records Management Software Applications Design Criteria Standard* has gone through several editions and is used by many organizations both within the US government and beyond.

National jurisdictions

Within individual countries there is often a range of formal standards, guidance and *de facto* standards. Most countries have a standards body that may have published records management standards in an area that the ISO or the International Council on Archives has not addressed. Also, many national governments, usually through the national archives, issue advice and guidance which acts as a *de facto* standard in that country for records management. Again, even if you do not work within government, advice and guidance of this type that is current practice in the public sector provides a model and checklist for how things can be done and is a useful touchstone against which to test your own systems.

An example of a national standard body with a relevant standard that ISO has not yet addressed is the British Standards Institute's **BIP 10008-1:2014:** *Evidential weight and legal admissibility of electronic information specification* and the related **BIP 0008-1:2014**: Code of Practice for the Implementation of BS 10008, which provides guidelines to ensure that digital records may be accepted as authentic records in a court of law.

An example of a *de facto* national standard is the DIRKS[3] ('designing and implementing recordkeeping systems') manual and methodology that was developed jointly by the National Archives of Australia and the State Records Authority of New South Wales. It draws on methodology used for the analysis and design of information technology to provide a modular approach to setting up records management programmes. It was developed at the same time as the Australian records management standard, an official Standards Australia publication, which was the inspiration for and basis of ISO 15489. ISO 15489 maps to the DIRKS methodology. The DIRKS steps are as follows:

- Step A – Preliminary investigation
- Step B – Analysis of business activity
- Step C – Identification of recordkeeping requirements
- Step D – Assessment of existing systems
- Step E – Identification of strategies for recordkeeping
- Step F – Design of a recordkeeping system
- Step G – Implementation of a recordkeeping system
- Step H – Post-implementation review.

We can see from this that the DIRKS approach and the one outlined in this book are very similar. Although no longer forming part of the National Archives of Australia's guidance package, DIRKS remains at the heart of New South Wales guidance. It is referred to extensively in the records management literature and used by other parts of the recordkeeping community.

Developing retention schedules

Figure 3.4 is a visual guide to how long different kinds of food can be kept in the freezer before it is unsafe to eat. Just as various kinds of frozen food have differing storage periods, so different types of record will vary in the length of time they should be kept before disposal.

A retention schedule is a timetable which specifies how long different kinds of records need to be kept before destruction or transfer to the archives. It sets out:

- the person or team responsible for the records
- the record type or series
- master or copy
- medium/format
- how long it has to be kept (this can be broken down into where it has to be kept, for example the office, storage away from the office)
- disposition (what needs to happen to it, destruction or transfer to the archives)
- the reason for the retention period.

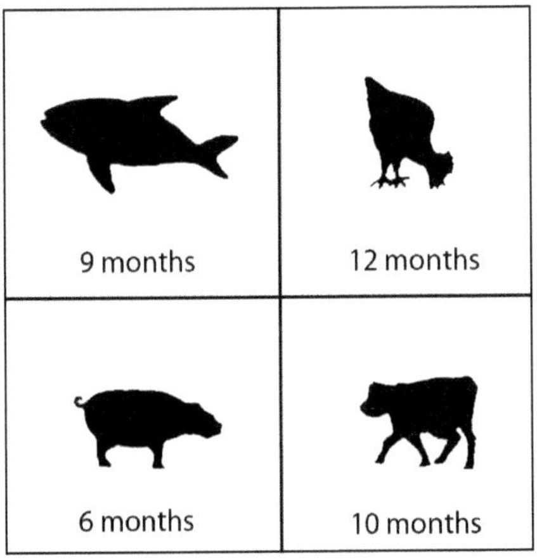

Figure 3.4 *Storing frozen food*

Constructing retention schedules

You will have noticed that the information in the retention schedule looks a lot like the data you collected during the record survey. Table 3.9 maps the data discussed in the section on surveying to the data required from the retention schedule.

Record appraisal work

The most challenging aspect of developing retention schedules, and of records management work in general, is deciding how long things should be kept and whether they are archival. We call this process 'appraisal'. It is important to take into account all of the factors affecting the value of the records in order to come to the right decision, but there is not always a clear indication of the time certain records need to be kept or whether they have archival value. Appraisal skills do, however, improve with practice and experience, so if you have an experienced records management colleague to consult, you should do so.

The first thing to remember is that, generally speaking, all the records in a series will need to be kept for the same length of time. Retention schedules therefore list the records by series. Checklist 3.4 gives some general guidance for appraising records.

Table 3.9 *Mapping the survey data to the retention schedules*

Original survey data	Retention schedule data
Interviewee, Interviewee's job title, Interviewee's department/section/team	The person or team responsible for the records
Which teams or individuals outside your own do you work and share records with?	
Who does the paper filing?	
Is there a shared team drive? (Ask for screen shots)	
Who creates the records?	
Who uses the records?	
Record series name	The record type or series
Medium or media	Medium/format
Are the records masters or copies?	Master or copy
Is the record series archival?	Disposition (what needs to happen to it, destruction or transfer to the archives)
When can the records be transferred to non-current storage?	Retention in office
Overall retention period before destruction/deletion	How long it has to be kept
Reason for the retention decision including any legislation which affects retention of the records	The reason for the retention period
Does the record series contain personal data?	

Checklist 3.4 General guidance for appraising records

- If the record series is the master, it must be kept as long as needed by anyone in the organization.
- Ask creators and users how they do their work and how long they need the records.
- Identify legislation that affects the work – and the records.
- Consider if the records might be useful to legally assert the organization's own position and rights and/or to protect it in the event of legal prosecution.
- Look at the retention schedules of other similar organizations, especially operational records.
- Use general retention guidance for administrative and corporate records.
- If the record provides key evidence for the history of the organization it may be archival: consult an archivist if possible.
- If the record is digital, it may be that it needs to be split for the retention schedule. For example, a database may be used to create reports that are important for management decision-making – the data itself may not be a record, or may not be needed for long, but the reports should be captured and retained, especially if the database is constantly being updated.
- If the record is a copy, it should be kept only as long as the user requires.
- If the series is information – printed matter or records and information from other organizations – retention should be as long as required.

A lot of general retention guidance is available on the internet and it is certainly worth studying. Two examples are:

1 The Archivist of the United States issues General Records Schedules (GRS) for US government departments to use. They authorize, after certain periods of time, destruction or transfer of records to the National Archives and Records Administration (NARA).
2 The National Archives in the UK issues standards for records management which consist mainly of retention guidance for commonly held administrative records in government departments. All of The National Archives standards have recently been brought together in a framework, available on its website.

It is worth noting that the guidance takes three main forms. The first kind tells you in general how long records arising from various functions should be kept, whereas the second specifies the record series. The third, most useful, combines the two. It can be difficult to relate the published guidance and retention schedules from other organizations to your own records. This is because all organizations are different, even if they do the same kind of thing: they may break the work down differently between departments and have different filing practices. For example, in some organizations the employment contracts are kept on separate files from the individual staff files and in others everything relating to one employee is kept on the same file. With the guidance above, it is easy for government bodies to follow because they probably have similar filing practices. Other organizations outside government might find it helpful to know what advice the leading government records managers are giving, but they may need to interpret, deconstruct or amalgamate elements to map it to their own record series.

Sample retention schedule

Figure 3.5 gives an example of a retention schedule in our imaginary MWC Ltd, so that you can see how it might look (remember it is just an example and the retention information is not applicable to all organizations).

It should be noted that this schedule gives guidance on how long to keep records in the office and in non-current storage. Another way to do it is to give an overall retention period as given in Figure 3.6. It is even possible to combine retention and disposition, as in the example in Figure 3.7.

It is important to be consistent in the way retention is expressed. It is also important to explain the way the retention instructions work. 'Current' might mean 'whilst employed', as in the example given here. It can also mean until the project is signed off, or the end of the financial year. The retention clock

Retention Schedule for Human Resources Department

Record series	Master or copy	Format	Retention in office	Retention in HR storage	Disposition	Authority
Job applications, unsuccessful	M	Paper	3 months	—	Destroy	In case of dispute, Data Protection (privacy)
Job applications, successful	M	Paper	Until appointed	—	Place on individual's HR file	
Individual HR files	M	Paper and digital	Until employment at Milson's ceases + 1 year	5 years	Destroy and delete from system	Statute of Limitations, Data Protection (privacy)
Annual leave records	M	Digital	2 years	—	Delete	Common practice
Attendance data: database	M	Digital	Keep current	—	Keep current	Agreed with Head of HR
Attendance data: management reports (from database)	M	Digital	Current + 1 year	5 years	Delete	Agreed with Head of HR
Budget files	C	Digital	2 years	—	Delete	Agreed with Head of Finance for all copy finance records
'The Human Resources Manager' magazine	C	Paper	As long as needed to refer to	—	Destroy	Information – not a Milson record

This schedule is authorized by:

Records Manager ____________________ Director of HR ____________________ Date: __________

Figure 3.5 *MWC Ltd retention schedule for human resources department*

Record series	Master or copy	Format	Overall Retention	Disposition	Authority
Individual HR files	M	Paper and digital	Current + 6 years	Destroy and delete from system	Statute of Limitations, Data Protection (privacy)

Figure 3.6 *MWC Ltd retention schedule entry, example A*

Record series	Master or copy	Format	Overall Retention Disposition	Authority
Individual HR files	M	Paper and digital	Destroy and delete from system	Statute of Limitations, Data Protection (privacy)

Figure 3.7 *MWC Ltd retention schedule entry, example B*

does not start to tick until the records are closed and no more are being added to the file or document folder. Therefore the retention period is applicable to all the records in the series, but the calculation has to be made based on the closing date of the records in question. It is important for us to be clear about this when we draft retention schedules, but it is even more important that we communicate it to people using the schedule.

Authorization and implementation

Establishing retention schedules is a linear process. We have covered much of the detail already, so here is a step-by-step guide:

1 Gather information on work done, record series and current retention practice.
2 Research other factors affecting retention, such as legislation, standards etc.
3 Draft retention schedules.
4 Consult end-users to confirm retention schedules.
5 Finalize retention schedules.
6 Get senior management authority for retention schedules.
7 Create guidance for using schedules, give training as needed.
8 End-users deal with record backlogs.
9 End-users establish cycle for regular review of records and action in line with schedules.

Non-current recordkeeping systems

Remembering that files in cabinets take up more space than boxed records, non-current records (those not needed frequently to support ongoing work) eventually fill up office storage space and computer drives. There are many risks associated with not managing these records, but the most compelling issue is that they impede access to the current records because they increase the search area. The logical thing to do is to remove them to non-current storage. However, if this is not done properly, it can result in uncontrolled growth of stashes of legacy records and information which cannot be accessed, can go missing, pose security and compliance risks and generally take up space unnecessarily.

One longstanding argument for records management is that it frees up office space, thus saving money both on records that could be destroyed and those that could be more cheaply stored elsewhere. This argument may be undermined if the office space is not more expensive than the alternative (plus any maintenance and retrieval costs), or if the records are predominantly digital. However, digital records storage also costs money and long-term preservation issues make their storage and maintenance expensive.

Physical storage space

Even with properly implemented retention schedules, office storage space may not be able to accommodate all the records. The records no longer needed constantly to support the work can be removed to storage which is cheaper and not so accessible. This may be in a part of the same building or building complex (for example the basement or attic) or offsite.

For records designated for destruction the minimum storage standard is lower than that for archives but there are a number of physical requirements to ensure that the space is well managed with respect to both physical protection and accessibility:

- Records should be in boxes to protect them from dirt and as a first-stage defence against fire and water incursion. The boxes can be as large as can be reasonably lifted.
- Boxes need to be on shelving: stacking boxes one on top of the other makes it hard to get at the boxes near the bottom, crushes the lower boxes and makes them vulnerable to water damage from flooding because water on the floor will wick up through the paper.
- Shelving needs to efficiently accommodate the boxes (or the boxes should fit on the shelves without wasteful gaps).
- Boxes may be shelved more than one deep and one high, depending on frequency of access.
- The shelving layout needs to make efficient use of the space, with aisle width to accommodate trolleys and ladders.
- It is best if the space does not have electric cables and water pipes running through it: fire extinguishers and mopping supplies should be kept handy.
- The door and all other access points to the space need to be kept locked and access limited to records management staff.
- There needs to be a workspace for records management staff to keep any paper documentation on the records and a computer, as well as to process and review retrieved records.
- Follow the health and safety regulations.

When deciding whether off-site storage is viable, you will need to weigh up the practical pros and cons as well as the financial ones. The distance from headquarters affects the speed and expense of retrieval. Decisions about going off-site and how far should be based on how quickly records need to be accessed at headquarters if needed, whether staff will be based at the storage and whether scanning and electronic transmission of records is a viable option. The general security of the area should also be taken into consideration. Being out of city centres can make premises less vulnerable to threats such as fire spreading from neighbouring buildings, civil unrest or terrorism. On the other hand, more isolated, less-frequented locations can be more vulnerable: criminals are less likely to be disturbed and other disasters may be undetected for a while.

If you decide it is not possible or practical to store the non-current records onsite, there are a number of additional requirements:

- There needs to be a loading bay so that records can be loaded into and removed from vehicles protected from the weather and in relative security.
- The staff workspace will need additional equipment, such as a phone line, scanner, printer and shredder.
- Staff need bathroom and eating facilities.
- There should be fire and flood alarms.
- Security should be very tight, with burglar alarms, CCTV and patrols as necessary.

It may be that your organization does not have appropriate off-site record storage available, or it would be more cost-effective to use a commercial record storage facility for non-current records. In that case, all of the requirements listed above need to be specified. You will also need to negotiate and manage the contract very carefully; in particular, these conditions need to be in place:

- All the records are always kept in the same storage area, which is dedicated to the organization's records.
- Contractors accessing the storage for maintenance purposes must log their activity.
- Otherwise, access is limited to records management staff.
- The contractor's performance is regularly reviewed.

It is not wise to let contractors take charge of finding aids and know the content of the records, partly for information security reasons and partly because if you do not maintain the finding aid yourself and you want to change contractors the data may be expensive to obtain and/or in a format that is not compatible with your organization's system.

In theory, once your records management programme is up and running, it should be possible for the records storage facility to get to the point where the amount of material coming in is equal to the amount going out for destruction. This presupposes that you are not keeping archival material in the same space.

Managing record content

Managing the physical aspects of non-current storage is important, but it is only half of the job. You also need to know the content of the boxes and where each box is in the storage facility. In order to do that you need to log key pieces of information about the records as they come in. You can do this for each individual file, although depending on the retention period and if this level of detail is needed to facilitate efficient retrieval, it is usually only necessary to do it for a group of records, either in the box, or a set of boxes with the same record series in it. For example, a set of staff leaver files for 2014 might come in three boxes and be organized within the box in alphabetical order by surname. If they are unlikely to be needed until they come due for destruction, they can be logged as a set. If there are more boxes, or there are already many boxes of leaver files, it might be necessary to list out the surnames. Regardless of the granularity required, the information should include:

- record owner (the person who created and used the records) and job title
- department
- file title (e.g., HR file: Fred Smith) or description of the group of files and how they are organized (e.g., HR leaver files: Anderson – Dwain)
- covering dates
- retention action date (e.g., destroy April 2019)
- confidentiality and/or access restrictions
- file or box reference
- location.

Ideally this information should be in a database, to facilitate not only searching but also sorting and reporting, for example by retention action, location or department, to support management of the facility. If this is not possible, a word-processed table is a good alternative.

It is not necessary for the records management team to gather and record all of this data. The record creators should be encouraged to provide this information when they transfer their records. This gives them more ownership of the records and awareness of the overhead necessary to manage them. You can provide them with forms to ensure all the necessary data is collected – and you can check the form before you accept the records to ensure they are transferring non-current records that need to be retained, with either a date for destruction or an archival designation. You can then enter the data into your system and supply the creator with a confirmation giving the file or box details and references.

It is not a good idea to put records with different retention action dates in the same box. It is much more efficient to have all the records needing destruction at the same time together, so that the retrieval and destruction process is efficient.

Metadata, indexing or keywords?

Metadata: literally 'data about data'; descriptive and other information about records to help understand, organize and manage them.

Index: set of alphabetized reference terms extracted from a record information resource to form a separate finding aid.

Keywords: agreed set of reference terms relevant to a record information resource which can be used to assist identification of relevant records.

The logging information outlined in the previous section will give record creators and users a good idea of what the records contain. For current and semi-current records management, this is the first priority. Sometimes it may be necessary to provide more detailed tagging, or metadata, about the records, to enable users to quickly identify the specific subject matter. Index terms and keywords allow users to quickly identify the records which mention or cover key subjects, locations or individuals.

However, indexing, keyword or thesaurus development and metadata schemas require consistency, attention to detail, the consensus of all concerned and a simple practical system that is easy to follow. For non-current records the cost in resources is often not worth the return, particularly as organizational users generally do not need it in order to access their records.

Providing access to records in non-current storage

Owners may still occasionally need to access non-current records and there needs to be a system in place to identify the records, log them out and return them afterwards. As discussed above, there should be a finding aid, perhaps a database, which identifies each record or group of records. The retrieved record must be logged out and the database will ideally accommodate this with a set of fields and a report option. The fields would include:

- record title and reference
- box reference
- location
- person requesting
- date retrieved
- date due
- date returned.

You can see the first three fields will be in the finding aid already. If many records are required you can generate a pick-list in location order. If you don't have a database, spreadsheets or tables are very effective.

When you have retrieved the records, return them to the requestor in a secure way, either by hand or through the internal mail. If the non-current storage is not on-site you may offer a copying facility to speed up the retrieval time. This might involve more records management staff time, as they will have to look for the exact document or pages needed. You need to decide if this service is necessary to support business needs and ensure people buy into the records management programme.

Finally, you need to ensure that the records come back once they have been used. You can then log them back in. It is not a good idea to erase the record of retrieval, because taken as a whole retrieval statistics will tell you a lot about how your service is being used. They can be used to justify the service and records management in general and/or they can show whether records are being transferred before they are non-current. Where records are not being accessed, there is evidence for reducing retention periods.

Digital storage

Although digital storage space may seem cheap compared with physical storage space it is not free and the contents can mount up, making the storage inefficient and unduly expensive. It is therefore important to ensure that all digital storage is managed carefully, records are kept securely, can be found and relied upon when needed and are not kept any longer than necessary. Depending on whether you have a digital records management system, you might need non-current storage for digital records. This would be for records which are not needed frequently to support ongoing work but need to be retained a while longer. The records management standards cited earlier will help you to draw up a list of requirements, particularly ICA-Req.

The space itself should ideally be a server housed in the organization's offices. Cloud computing solutions can also be used, whereby the organization purchases access to a service which includes hosting, software and back-up which can be accessed from anywhere in the world.

As with analogue storage (and indeed current digital records), the records need to be secure from unauthorized access and malevolent or accidental change or deletion. Non-current digital records must be locked down so that no changes can be made by anyone. Whilst end-users may directly access records, if the records in the repository come from a variety of organizational areas a range of access permissions is required. Managing security properly protects records that need it whilst ensuring authorized people can access the relevant records.

Once you have created the secure space, you will need to consider the best format for the records. Chapter 5 covers digital preservation issues, so we will not rehearse them here. The important thing is that your preservation strategy and processes ensure records will be accessible and reliable until they are destroyed.

Retrieving digital records, so that end-users can consult a record or group of records, will depend on the quality of the metadata (information about the records). This can be challenging to achieve with digital records because end-users often think full-text retrieval will be good enough. The information listed above on managing record content provides a good basis for the metadata necessary for digital records in non-current storage. One of the potential benefits of digital recordkeeping is that end-users can retrieve and access records for themselves. The system should maintain an audit trail of access events, for the same reasons as statistics are kept on the use of paper records in non-current systems.

One of the crucial pieces of metadata is the retention period and it is vital that records are deleted accordingly. The next section describes how to do this, but remember that digital records are backed up and copied so it is important to have a way to ensure that all copies and back-ups are also deleted.

Disposal

> **Disposal:** ultimate fate of a record, either destruction or transfer to the archive.

Disposal is the last phase of the record's lifecycle. It is not a euphemism for 'destruction' but a word to cover two possibilities. Both options require an appraisal framework which has been established early in the records' lifecycle and appropriate documentation to demonstrate compliance for destroyed records and to ensure ongoing reliability and access for archives.

Records in offices or non-current storage need to be managed to identify those that are reaching their retention date or those that need to be transferred to the archives. This can be done by sorting metadata tables, running reports in databases or automatic alerts generated by electronic records management systems.

If this final task is not carried out, the whole records management process is undermined. It can also be very satisfying, as it is the culmination of all the organization and assessment work that has been done before.

Destruction

There are a variety of ways to destroy records in and on physical media, including:

- shredding or cutting down to a specified particle size
- burning to ash
- melting down
- chemical or mechanical treatment to destroy the recorded surface
- pulping.

The method of destruction will depend on financial constraints, the sensitivity of the information and the risks around not properly eliminating the records. For non-sensitive paper records the best thing is to shred and then the shredding can be recycled. For sensitive paper records they need to be shredded and pulped or burned in a fast process, preferably in-house. If you are not destroying in-house you need to specify the contract very carefully, to ensure that records are secure during transport, do not get stored before destruction and that they are actually destroyed. You should require a certificate of destruction and periodically travel with the waste material to audit the process.

Regardless of whether the destruction takes place in-house or is contracted out, the documentation required is the same and consists of:

- list of records destroyed
- extract of relevant retention schedule
- authorization by end-user and/or manager plus records manager
- certificate of destruction.

With digital records residing in a non-current records repository such as is described in the previous section, it is more difficult to destroy the records. This is because often all you can do is destroy the route to the record whilst the record itself remains on the disk until the space is needed, and even then computer experts can still read it. Also, there will be back-ups which are not usually organized in such a way that identification of individual or groups of records is easy – so even if you know where all the back-ups are, you might not be able to find the specific records. Records managers also need to be aware that some finance and HR software will not allow records to be deleted, which means they are not good recordkeeping systems.

Transfer to the archives

As we know, some records have ongoing value because they provide evidence for the history of the organization and/or society. These records should have been identified during the record survey process and ideally, as soon as they cease to be needed to do current work, they will have gone straight to the archives. Archival storage is more stringent in terms of physical environmental factors and security than storage for records that will eventually be destroyed.

Because archives are kept for ever, it is crucial to have the component records well organized and documented. In addition to the list of logging information mentioned before, a description of the records series and the work from which it arises is very useful. Also, it is very important not to lose the organization of the records, which can easily happen, for example by mixing records from different departments or different record series. Thus, the documentation should consist of a list of records transferred with all the necessary metadata, together with the extract from the retention schedule or collecting policy that designates the records as archival and contact details for the creator or end-user.

Management of archival records and storage is covered in Chapter 4.

Managing vital records

In the context of records management the term 'vital records' has a very specific meaning. It is those records which, in the event of an emergency, are essential to carry on business. The vital records programme ensures that they have been identified, are protected and available when needed. I have already mentioned that identifying vital records can be part of the records and information survey: managing them is definitely part of the records management programme. As vital records management is also part of emergency planning, I am going to cover the initial identification and management aspects here, but we will leave the larger function of preventing, preparing for and recovering from disasters for Chapter 5.

Identification

Although end-users can help in identification, they often understand vital records to be the ones that are necessary to do their job, when they are in reality those which are crucial for ongoing business. Therefore, it is necessary to specify what aspects of the organization's business would be crucial in the event of a disaster before identifying the supporting records. This will depend upon the business, but to establish the vital activity, you must work with all areas of the organization. Ultimately the decision about what is vital business should be made at the highest level in the organization and this will determine the set of vital records. The following types of records are usually candidates for inclusion in the vital records register:

- insurance records
- financial records proving payment or monies owing
- employee records for the current pay cycle
- records establishing operating rights, giving details of contracts and protecting against litigation
- key operational records such as contact lists, research, engineering drawings, formulae
- physical, financial and intellectual property ownership records
- incorporation records and board minutes
- manuals and codes for systems necessary in emergencies, such as elevators, alarm systems and staff contact lists.

It is important to remember that the number of vital records is small – only 2–4% of the overall number of records. If records are mistakenly identified as vital the programme will be difficult to operate. Also note that archival records are not necessarily vital to the ongoing operation of the business.

Whilst vital records should be surveyed and noted with other records as part of establishing the records management programme, we need extra information about vital records in order to protect and manage them efficiently. It may be necessary to do a separate, more detailed, survey of vital records to find out:

- volume and rate of accumulation
- storage media
- activity or function record supports
- how long it remains current
- frequency of use.

Protecting vital records

Once all the vital records have been identified you will be able to use the additional information to work out a protection plan. Protection is about finding a way to ensure that the record, or the information or evidence in the record, is still available after a disaster. Obviously the best protection is ensuring that the disaster does not happen, and we will cover this in Chapter 5, but however good your preventative measures are the risk will always be there. Another option is to ensure that the vital records are protected by additional security measures such as keeping them in fire-proof safes – although the risks still remain that it might be cracked or damaged, thus threatening the records. The last option is to copy the records and keep the master or original off-site. In order to copy vital records you need to establish a copying programme, although it may be possible to rely in part on the regular distribution of copies of records around the organization. Digital vital records can easily be copied. Paper records will require a process to copy in paper or scan to digital media or microform. It takes time to retrieve copies from off-site locations and the copying programme requires consistency and attention to detail from the end-users, as well as from records management staff.

In deciding what strategy to pursue, you need to consider the cost in conjunction with the level of risk. For example, the older board minutes (bound into volumes) are a vital record because they provide evidence of the decision-making process of senior executives and stockholders (and are also archival, but that is not why they are vital). The need to retrieve and use the older minutes in the event of an emergency is minimal, so making good quality microform copies is an excellent solution. Microform does not require a high level of preservation management, as it can survive for a long time in a stable environment without any intervention. If a disaster destroys the master set of minutes the microform copies can be used to print out a paper copy, or to create a set of PDFs, once the immediate crisis has been dealt with. Staff payroll records, however, may be needed quite soon after the emergency. Assuming the accounting software package, with all the records going back for at least six years, may well be down and any back-up restoration will take a significant amount of time, a report of the current and last payroll period could be backed up separately as, for example, a spreadsheet. It could even be printed out. Therefore, you need to take into account the need to access the copy records in an emergency. Paper may be best, since other media require equipment and a power source to be read. Table 3.10 gives the three main strategies with risk level and financial considerations.

Tracking vital records

At the end of the process of identifying and selecting protection measures for vital records you will be able to develop a list or register giving management information. Table 3.11 gives an example.

As with any records in storage, be they current filing, non-current, archival or back-up, there needs to be a finding aid of some description to support

Table 3.10 *Vital record protection strategies*

Strategy	Measures	Risk level	Cost factors
Prevent disaster from happening	Good cyber- and physical security; fire and flood prevention	High	Should be part of organization's disaster plan
Protect original from adverse event	Place in safe, fire-proof cabinets, waterproof containers	Less high	May entail additional expenditure
Have back-up copy	Copy and send copy off-site	Lowest	Managing the programme is an ongoing overhead

Table 3.11 *Sample vital records register*

Department	Record Type	Vital activity	Media	Volume	Accrual rate	Currency	Protection	Notes
Human resources	Payroll	Managing workforce remuneration	Digital	2 Excel folders	1 Excel folder per month	Only keep current and previous month	Back up Vital Records server	Need to extract from Payroll system
Chief executive	Board minutes	Corporate decision-making	Paper	10 volumes, 3 folders	1 thin folder per month	Must keep all	Scan backlog to PDF, keep PDF of all documents going forward – all reside on Vital Records server	Signed master remains in paper format

retrieval and to manage the holdings. Vital record holdings should be logged and managed in the same way as other records. The programme should include processes to ensure that the records are sent off site in a timely fashion, they are clearly labelled and logged to ensure that they can be found quickly if needed, they are destroyed or deleted when their currency as vital records expires and this is recorded in the finding aid. The finding aid itself needs to be available to the disaster recovery team, as well as to the records manager, in digital as well as hard-copy formats.

Recall and reconstitution

If there is a disaster and the organization's records are destroyed or cannot be accessed, the vital records recovery procedures come into play. The records may be used *in situ* at the storage facility, but they may need to come back to a central location. Filing systems, either paper or electronic, need to be set up and populated with the records and there may be a need to generate different formats of the records. From a recordkeeping perspective the important thing in all of this activity, which will probably be conducted under great pressure, is to remember that the records need to be kept as securely as possible and the transportation and copying processes should be documented.

Digital records

As mentioned before, the choice of record format can affect accessibility in the event of a disaster. Digital records require hardware, software and a power source for access, so depending on the disaster, it might not be the best medium for copies of vital records. However, the fact that everything on an organization's system is generally backed up by the IT team as a matter of course does mean that it should be possible to locate many vital records sooner or later. Whilst it is not good to rely on the routine back-up, which takes time to reconstitute and will not be designed to streamline access to vital records, in the longer term it will mean that all areas of the organization will be able to resume where they left off, if the vital business operations have been able to keep going.

There are other ways that modern technology could be of benefit to the vital records programme. Hand-held devices and laptop computers have huge storage capacity these days, so it would be possible to reconstitute filing systems on small personal computing equipment. Also cloud computing, which, as we have seen, allows you to access your records from anywhere in the world, may offer a good solution, allowing you to scan vital records directly into an organized storage area in the cloud.

Handling legacy records

> **Legacy records:** old or non-current records which have been dumped or accumulated in storage spaces, and which have not been subject to recent records management action. The record creators may be gone from the organization or unknown.

Accumulations of old, disorganized records can be very daunting for end-users, who will need help to manage them. The record survey and retention schedule development exercises will have revealed any stashes of records, in both paper and digital formats. The paper will most commonly be in a cupboard or a basement, which may also harbour caches of floppy disks or other digital media. Legacy digital records may also be lurking on the system in folders that belonged to a departed colleague or a drive belonging to a department that has since been reorganized out of existence.

Dealing with legacy records takes time, of course, and can either be blitzed or tackled in shorter regular sessions over a period of time. It requires a systematic approach and some guidelines, to ensure that the records of continuing business value are retained and listed so as to be accessible, as well as tagged with a retention action date. Similarly, archive records need to be identified and subject to archive management policy. Finally, all the other records need to be destroyed and the destruction (or deletion) documented as outlined in the section on destruction above.

If there is no urgent need to clear space or access particular records, it is best to leave the legacy record clean-up project until after the new records management system is in place. The priority is to manage the records well going forward. Once there is time to deal with the legacy records, the work done to set up the new system will really help. Before looking at the records in detail, gather the relevant documentation, such as the survey findings, the retention schedules and any lists of the records. Checklist 3.5 is an action plan for dealing with legacy records.

Checklist 3.5 Action plan for dealing with legacy records

1 Use any existing lists to identify relevant retention schedule guidance that can be applied to the records.
2 If there are no lists carry out an inventory of the records, marking them with a preliminary retention assessment (archive, retain for *x* years, destroy immediately).
3 Draw up list of records for destruction, attach to retention schedule guidance and destroy/delete records.
4 Transfer archival records to the archives or make sure they are separated from the other records and housed in archive boxes.
5 Turn record inventory into a finding aid to manage record storage, as outlined earlier in this chapter in the section on non-current storage.
6 Box records with the same destruction date together to make the process as easy as possible.

Initial review and ongoing audit

Once the new records management programme is up and running it should be reviewed within 6–12 months to ensure that end-users are managing their records and the system works. The best way to do this is to carry out a mini-survey and to revisit your original interviewees to ask them a set of questions designed to assess their engagement with the system, whether it works for them and if anything needs to be changed to make it work better. The kind of questions to ask are:

- How is the new paper filing system working? If it is not good, what are the issues?
- How is the new digital folder structure working? If it is not good, what are the issues?
- Have you dealt with the legacy records – if not, why not?
- How are the non-current records being managed?
- Have you been using the retention schedules, and how are you finding them? Does anything need to be added or subtracted?
- Are you finding records easily? Are records being replaced correctly where they came from?

It is a good idea to get people to show you both paper filing systems and digital folders so you can see the system in action.

Records management is like gardening or hairdressing: everything looks great immediately after the lawn has been mown or the highlights put in but with the passage of time everything tends to revert to a messier state. This is partly because of human nature but also because organizations change and reorganize, and with these changes departments or teams have different functions – and the records they create and use will be different. That is why, after the first review, it is important to carry out audits every two years or so, or after an organizational restructure. The audit should be fairly rigorous and it is good to draw up a detailed audit checklist, perhaps using the international standard as a basis, or at least going back to your original records management project plan to ensure that you cover every aspect of the programme. Checklist 3.6 gives a list of records management elements to investigate together with suggestions for checking they are being properly managed.

Checklist 3.6 Records management audit questions

Adherence to policies and procedures

- Are staff aware of the various policies?
- Are they following the procedures, allowing for local variations?

Compliance with legislation, regulation and standards

- How are records containing personal data handled?
- Is the level of records management sufficient to ensure compliance with FoI?
- Is records management meeting industry-specific requirements?

Implementation of retention schedules

- Are the retention schedules used?
- Are there records of destroyed or deleted records?

- Does the retention schedule still cover all the records?
- Are the retention times still correct?

Non-current recordkeeping systems: storing, documenting, retrieving and tracking records

- What does the physical space look like?
- Is the finding aid fit for purpose?
- Are records that have been checked out being chased and returned?

Disposal

- How is destruction being carried out?
- Are there records of destroyed or deleted records?
- What happens to archives?

Managing vital records and planning for disaster

- How is the vital records programme working?
- Is the vital records list up to date?
- Is the recovery plan tested regularly?

Legacy systems

- What documentation is there on the legacy records?
- Is there an ongoing project to clean up legacy records?

As a result of the audit survey you will be able to adjust the records management programme accordingly. You may also need to do some more awareness raising and training.

Round-up

This chapter is the longest one in the book because a comprehensive records management regime requires a thorough understanding of the organization, its work and records – as well as a number of policies and processes to ensure that good records are created, are reliable, remain accessible yet secure, and are either destroyed or preserved as archives when no longer needed to support current business. Long as it is, this chapter also shows that records management also breaks down into a series of steps or processes that, if followed through with sensitivity to your colleagues' work goals, will ensure that you can establish effective recordkeeping for your organization.

Notes

1 *Chambers 20th Century Dictionary.*

2 www.iso.org/iso/home/store/catalogue_tc/catalogue_tc_browse.htm?commid=48856.

3 www.records.nsw.gov.au/recordkeeping/advice/designing-implementing-and-managing-systems.

CHAPTER 4

Archives management

Introduction

The definition of archives given in Chapter 1 is 'records of one organization, family or individual, selected for permanent preservation because they provide key evidence of the entity's history'. Chapter 1 also covered the various media that records – and therefore archives – come in, the different types of archive repositories, what working with archives involves and the wider context, together with sources of information and support. It also gave an overview of what archive users and researchers might be looking for in the archives. This chapter will build on the concepts and principles articulated in Chapter 1, continuing to follow the journey of archival records as they move away from the main body of records that will be destroyed and begin to be managed differently and separately in order to safeguard them for posterity.

In managing archives we are seeking to keep a comprehensive record, which provides the evidence of what happened and why, for the future, for ever. This requires the identification of a set of documentation which gives the history of the individual, family, organization or community. We also need to look after them in a way that gives them the best possible chance of surviving the ravages of the environment and human interference over time. It also requires making the records available, publicizing their existence and interpreting them to make them more accessible to more people. These three aspects of managing archives all need to be in place to do the job properly, but it is also important to be able to advocate and justify the resources expended, because caring for archives over time is an expensive proposition.

Chapter 4 is organized to follow the work process that needs to be in place to manage archives from the time we first start to think about taking archives into custody. It does not cover preservation, the aspect of managing archives which addresses the archives' accommodation, environment and handling procedures in order to preserve them, as this is treated separately in Chapter 5. We start with the collecting policy which dictates the overall content of the archive, through acquisition of archives and accessioning or logging them in. Then the process of archival appraisal is covered, which ensures that we take the comprehensive record and discard the records that are not adding to the story. This is followed by arrangement and description, where we document the organization of and relationships between the records and develop summaries of the contents of the records. Then we discuss the different types of finding aids that might need to be created in order to manage and access the archives. Providing access to archives is then explored, followed by how to work effectively with volunteers.

Collecting policies

> **Archive collecting policy:** description of the broad scope and content of the repository's holdings, as is and as envisioned in the future, used to inform acquisition of new material.

In Chapter 1, we mentioned the need for people working in archives to know about collecting policy and the high-level decision-making process around determining what archives to acquire. The archive collecting policy (sometimes called the acquisition policy) is a key management tool that sets out which kinds of material the repository holds, why and the authority for it. It is crucial to demonstrate the archive is being run according to best practice. For example, in the UK The National Archives sets out specific requirements for collecting policies as part of the Archive Service Accreditation Standard, the quality assurance scheme for British archives. The collecting policy determines the overall content of the archive, allows for a logical and efficient approach to acquisitions work, and provides all stakeholders with a clear indication of what sort of material is in the archives and is likely to be acquired in the future. It can be used to match organizational and archival aims to available resources. It is the initial high-level appraisal tool, setting the framework for specific decisions on what archives the repository will accept. It allows the archivist to be in control of the content of the archive. In addition, a collecting policy offers benefits in improving the consistency and objectivity of archive acquisition decision-making, as follows:

- objective, consistent decision-making over time by different individuals
- assessment of value of potential acquisitions in context
- efficient, targeted use of resources for storage, preservation and use functions, in accordance with organizational and archival aims
- co-operation with other repositories, as appropriate
- donors can identify the best repository for their archive
- diplomatic refusal of unsuitable materials
- identification of gaps in the holdings
- representative and comprehensive development of holdings
- reappraisal and de-accessioning.

In drafting the collecting policy, there are a number of factors to consider. Checklist 4.1 lists the questions to be asked.

Checklist 4.1 Drafting the collecting policy

- What are you trying to achieve in creating and maintaining the repository?
- What are the goals of your parent organization?
- What are the repository's current resources, and in the future?
- What kinds of records, from which creators, does the repository currently hold?
- What are the strengths and weaknesses of the current archive holdings?
- How do the archives from different provenances complement one another?
- Is there secondary supporting documentation (books, periodicals, databases)?
- What are the collecting policies of other repositories in the same or related subject areas – will your policy be competitive or complementary?
- What are the trends in research and scholarship, both in your repository and more widely in the subject area?

When you have gathered information on the current situation, you can analyse it and start to draft the policy. The policy needs to include certain elements, most of which are factual and will be straightforward to document. The most difficult bit is drafting the collecting scope, the unique and detailed description of what kind of records have been and will be acquired. This could be centred on a geographical area, such as state or local government archives, or concerned with a specific subject or theme, for example military history. It might be limited to the organization's own archives, support the research interests of a group of stakeholders, or be media-specific, for example a film archive. The scope indicates what the archives aspires to document and you should aim to couch it in terms of the subjects, functions or activities of which the records provide evidence. Remembering the concept of collecting archives, where records from a variety of different organizations are brought together, it stands to reason that collecting policies need to work for archives which aim solely to document the history of one creating entity as well as archives which take in records from a few or many different provenances. Policies for collecting archives tend to focus on the likely activity of the creators of desirable records. If you find you are getting to the level of describing specific record series, the policy is too detailed and will be difficult to implement, possibly excluding records you want and allowing those you don't. Archive collecting policies should cover the subjects listed in Checklist 4.2. Figure 4.1 gives a collecting policy, adapted from a real example, mapped to this checklist.

Repository Details The Theatro Technis Archive Theatro Technis Limited 26 Crowndale Road London NW1 1TT	Information identifying the repository – and its governing body
Collecting Authority The Theatro Technis Board approved the decision to establish the Archive at its regular meeting in December 2009. Theatro Technis is not covered by any specific archive legislation but complies with Data Protection legislation. The Archive was set up with the help of a Heritage Lottery Fund grant. The archive aims to document the work of Theatro Technis and provide evidence of its history.	The repository's legal status and source of its authority to collect The repository's mission
Scope of Collecting Policy The Archive seeks to collect records which document the life and experience of the Cypriot immigrant community in London through the theatre and its community advisory, support and campaigning activities which forged lasting links with the wider theatre community and neighbouring London groups with common interests. Priority will be given to records documenting the life of immigrants from the geographic boundary of Camden and to records relating to Theatro Technis activities, including but not restricted to: • records documenting the administration, promotion and performance of Theatro Technis productions • records documenting the use of the theatre by visiting theatre companies • theatre scripts of plays performed by the Theatro Technis theatre company • records of Theatro Technis' community advisory service • records of Theatro Technis' campaigning activities • records documenting Theatro Technis' anniversaries and celebrations • oral and written history and biography of individuals connected with Theatro Technis. The Archive will consider collecting archives in all media, including modern media such as electronic records and audio-visual recordings.	The collecting scope

Figure 4.1 *Theatro Technis Archive: archive collecting policy (adapted from the company's policy with permission)* *(Continued on facing page)*

Checklist 4.2 Contents of a collecting policy

- Information identifying the repository – and its governing body
- The repository's legal status and source of its authority to collect
- The repository's mission
- The collecting scope
- Co-operation with other repositories
- Acquisition conditions, including ownership, transfer of intellectual property rights, financial arrangements and access restrictions
- Exclusions to the policy, including non-archival material such as artefacts and supporting documentation, arrangements for disposal
- Procedures for exceptions to the policy
- Date of policy and review.

Co-operation with other repositories Where the Theatro Technis collecting policy overlaps with the collecting policy of other archives, we will work with other interested parties to ensure that the material is deposited with the most appropriate body.	Co-operation with other repositories
Acquisition Theatro Technis seeks to acquire records either as a loan pending copying of the records or as outright gifts wherever possible. No records will be accepted without an Archives Donation/Loan Agreement. Theatro Technis is not in a position to purchase archive material. Wherever possible Theatro Technis works to establish intellectual property rights, and in particular seeks to acquire the right to copy archival material for preservation and access purposes. Unless specifically limited under Data Protection legislation, all material in the Theotro Technis archives will be open to access by bona fide researchers according to the archive access policy. Where records are damaged and require extensive conservation and preservation resources, it may only be possible for Theatro Technis to take them if funding is available to ensure their physical preservation. Archives acquired by Theatro Technis will, subject to the Archives Donation/Loan Agreement, be retained and preserved permanently. However, Theatro Technis Archive shall, in accordance with the wishes and requirements of depositors, evaluate and select documents considered not to be worthy of permanent preservation. Such records will be offered back to the depositor before any destruction.	Acquisition conditions including ownership, transfer of intellectual property rights, financial arrangements and access restrictions Exclusions to the policy
Exceptions Records which do not match this Policy may exceptionally be acquired, if there is a clear relationship with the activity of Theatro Technis. This may be done with the agreement of the Archives manager and the Chief Executive.	Exceptions to the policy
Date of Issue and Review Date of policy: 20th December 2014 This policy is due for review: December 2017	

Figure 4.1 *Continued*

With a sound collecting policy, you can begin to develop your archive holdings in a planned and pro-active way, rather than being passive and waiting for potential donations to come in. Organizational archives now have a clear remit to take in the archival records from other areas of the business or institution, and they can use the policy to review holdings and identify areas where records have not been transferred. As already mentioned, the policy can be used to review existing holdings and ensure that they all meet the criteria. For collecting archives, the policy can be used to help identify organizations that may be creating the kind of archives the repository is interested to acquire.

Acquisition

As briefly outlined in Chapter 1, we need to ensure that custody and ownership (physical and intellectual) and access rights of the archive holdings are clear. This can be a complicated aspect of managing archives, for three reasons:

1 Archive holdings can be very old and their acquisition may not have been recorded.
2 They may be found (in skips, for example), lent, donated or purchased.
3 Intellectual property rights can be difficult to establish and may not reside with the individual depositing the material.

Managing the acquisition process involves using a collecting policy to negotiate with potential depositors to come to a mutually acceptable outcome, documented in an acquisition agreement. Before embarking on the negotiations, it is important to ensure that the records fit into the collecting policy and that the person or organization offering them is entitled to do so.

> **Depositor:** individual giving or lending the archives to the repository.

> **Donation:** outright gift of archive materials.

> **Loan:** archives lodged with the archives for permanent custody without transfer of legal ownership.

With archives that have been in the repository for many years and for which there is no documentary trail, the best you can do is try to research their origin and establish the intellectual property rights – and document your actions and findings. The same applies to archives which have been found, or anonymously donated.

It is not ideal to have a lot of archives in the repository that are lent, rather than donated outright. This is because the owner – or the owner's heirs – can always withdraw them. We discussed in the previous section the need for a collecting policy that can in turn inform a collections/holdings development strategy. From this perspective every single archive in the repository will have been carefully selected and matched to the criteria. Furthermore, considerable resources are required to look after archives, including: space on shelves; archival quality containers; expertise to describe; conservation measures. Therefore any acquisition agreement must have a clause that protects the repository from withdrawal of archives.

The best way for a repository to acquire archives is through outright gift. The archives are donated, together with intellectual property rights, and the repository is free to manage and use them as appropriate. Another way to acquire archives is through purchase. This will be documented with a sales catalogue and a receipt for the material. Finally, archives may be acquired as a transfer from another part of the organization. It won't be necessary to have an agreement contract about these transferred records, but they will need to be documented and logged into the repository, as outlined in Chapter 3.

Acquisition agreements

The acquisition agreement ensures that we have secure custody of the archives accessioned into the repository and the repository has clear rights to manage and use the material. It may be appropriate to take legal advice on the form and detail of the acquisition agreement that you use, but generally, the agreement needs to cover the points listed in Checklist 4.3.

Checklist 4.3 Points to cover in an acquisition agreement

- Identity of the person or organization transferring the archives
- Identity of the owner of the archives
- Identity of the owner of any intellectual property rights residing in the archives
- Identification of repository as new owner or custodian of the archives
- Assignment of any intellectual property rights and applicable conditions
- Clear description of the archives, the quantity and content
- Agreed access permissions and restrictions
- Conditions around disposal of material that is non-archival
- The repository's undertaking to care for the archives
- Date of agreement, names and positions of signatories.

Where the archives are being lent to the repository, there need to be additional clauses covering:

- financial compensation to the repository for storing, preserving, cataloguing and providing access
- the right to make copies of the archive as a surrogate for the original.

Intellectual property rights for archives

We do not have time to go into intellectual property rights management for archives in detail, especially as the rights vary from country to country. However, there are a few issues to be aware of which impact on the management of archives and ideally should be addressed at the point of acquisition. Intellectual property rights encompass copyright, patents and trademarks, as well as others which are not so relevant for archives. The right of the creator to use and distribute the work, invention or design is protected, usually for a set period of time, in law. These rights may vary according to the kind of work. For example, published works, unpublished works and sound recordings are dealt with differently under the UK Copyright, Designs and Patents Act of 1988. Intellectual property rights may be inherited or assigned and they are separable from ownership of the physical original or publication (think of a book that you own, which you have no right to copy and distribute). There also may be several rights owners, for example with films, where the director, screenplay author and composer each have rights, or with correspondence, where the person in receipt of the letters or e-mail is not the creator. In some cases the creator will not have the primary rights: for example, where the product is created by the employee of an organization the organization will hold the primary rights. Intellectual property rights may also cover the content of a database.

The most obvious way in which intellectual property rights impact archives is in providing our users with copies of records. However, there are some other equally significant aspects of our work which are impacted. It is sometimes necessary to make copies of archives for preservation purposes, for example to create a surrogate because the original is too fragile to use. With digital and audiovisual archives, not only does the original need to be copied (or indeed digitized, if it is an analogue recording) for routine preservation reasons, but the software may need to be copied or kept beyond the licence agreement. Many audiovisual archives record broadcasts and transmissions as part of their acquisition process and providing access to audiovisual holdings may also involve a broadcast or showing of the material, both of which will require rights permissions. Archive repositories may wish to use excerpts from the archives in exhibitions and publications. All of these are legally possible, either under exceptions to the law (such as the UK fair dealing clause, which allows limited copying for private study, disabled accessibility, reporting or teaching purposes), under a licensing agreement or through permission from the rights owner.

It is best to establish an intellectual property policy, which will feed into the acquisition process, as well as ongoing management of the archives. Here are a few pointers to follow:

- identify material subject to intellectual property rights, the owner(s) and duration
- assess the impact of those rights on management of the archives
- seek to acquire rights to use the material in order to preserve and make

it available
- if you cannot find the rights owners, you may still be able to use the archives as needed for preservation and access – but document your investigative work
- you may need expert advice.

Remember also that in managing archives we need to take the long view and intellectual property law, by limiting the duration of rights, recognizes the public right of access to cultural heritage in the longer term. However, it may also be that the limitations of the intellectual property rights incumbent on the archives in question make acquisition of the material undesirable.

Accessioning

> **Accession:** group of records received into the archive repository from a single creator at the same time.

Accessioning is the initial registration of archives into the repository and acts as a control giving essential details about the totality of records received from that provenance at that time. The accession records as a whole provide data about the holdings which is essential for global management of the archives, particularly if the records are from external sources. Archival records from within the parent organization are identified in the retention schedule as archives and are usually well organized and documented. All of this was noted in previous chapters, but regardless of how the records are acquired, the accessioning process and documentation is the same.

The accessions register

Traditionally archivists kept a formal bound volume to record incoming records, usually with neatly ruled columns that were filled out in indelible ink. These days it is more common to find a digital equivalent, still referred to as an accessions register. Archive management software may have an accessions module for this purpose. The accessions register contains a profile of information about all the records in the repository. It is the first step in establishing control over the content of the archives. It describes what they are about, informing the more detailed cataloguing work which cannot usually be done immediately and provides a basic inventory of all of the holdings. Table 4.1 gives a list of accession data with a sample entry and explanatory notes.

Table 4.1 *Accession data and sample entry*

Data	Sample entry	Notes
Unique accession number	2015/002	Using the current year and a running number is common practice for archives
Date of acquisition/entry	15 January 2015	Sometimes the records will be acquired before the accession is entered in the register
Title	Records of the Somers Town Community Theatre	This is simply a handy name for the material
Amount of material	10 record boxes	This is needed to ensure that all parts of the accession are identified
Details of depositor or vendor	James Smith, Theatre Manager, Somers Town Community Theatre, 15 Chalton Street, London N1	This could be a colleague, a private individual, someone working for or on behalf of the creating organization, or a vendor such as an auction house
Creator	Somers Town Community Theatre	Documenting provenance is crucial for both authenticity and understanding the records
Terms of deposit	Gift, some access restrictions for data protection (see acquisition agreement)	This is for recording the type of deposit – gift, loan, purchase, transfer – as well as any specific access restrictions
Covering dates	January 2006–December 2010	This can sometimes only be a rough guide, to be amended when more detailed cataloguing work is done
Summary description	Records of the Theatre Board, Box Office, Prop Department, Script Library and Marketing Departments. See accession file for detailed lists of some of these record groups	This is a brief description of the content of the archives being transferred – it can be useful to refer to any lists or finding aids that came with the records
Media	Paper and CD-ROMs	This is useful to manage preservation needs
Accruals	This is an accrual to the STCT archive, further accruals are expected	Records material from the same provenance as existing holdings and if more records are expected
Final reference		If different references are used for catalogued material

Accession files

You will almost certainly need to set up a series of accessions or acquisitions files to hold all of the documentation relating to the accession or the record group. Remember that whilst an accession may be the entire archive of a dead person or an organization that is no longer operating, it is also possible that an accession is only part of the entire archive. Depending on the type of archive repository you are managing, you may need a file for each archive or a file for each accession. The accession file might contain the acquisition agreement, any list or other finding aid for the records, correspondence with the depositor, the purchase receipt or any other background information relevant to the archive.

Retrospective accessioning

If you are starting out and have inherited the archive without accessions documentation, you could fill out an accessions register retrospectively. Your first priority is to establish control of all the new material that comes in, to maintain order going forwards. Once you've set up the register and accessioning procedures, use the same fields to structure an audit form to collect information about the un-accessioned material. You need to find out as much information as you can about where the material has come from and you may find this in depositors' correspondence, deposits recorded in the organization's minutes, or organizational memory of staff and retired employees. Use the inventory and research findings to populate the accessions register. This is the beginning, even if there are gaps in the details, of knowing what archives you have and planning their management.

Appraisal

> **Appraisal:** assessment of records to determine their value as primary source material providing evidence of the history of the organization, family or individual.

The definition of archives we are using in this book states they are '*selected* for permanent preservation because they provide key evidence of the entity's history'. The process of selecting archives, or 'appraisal', is a crucial aspect of managing archives. We cannot keep every record, because even if we had the space, we would not have the resources to catalogue and preserve them – but we also do not need to keep everything. What we need to keep is the discrete set of records which provide the evidence, and therefore the story, of the organization, family, individual or community. As we mentioned in Chapter 3, we also appraise current and semi-current records in order to assign time periods prior to destruction. With archival appraisal there are two options, to keep or not to keep, and our choice must ensure that we keep the key records and destroy those that do not materially add to the story.

For organizational archives subject to records management it is likely that records transferred from departments are reliably archival. For most other kinds of accessions, it will be necessary to undertake appraisal. Whilst there are some principles to follow, the precise set of records forming the archive will vary from case to case. Appraisal practice combines knowledge of those principles with knowledge of the organization and its records. Appraisal skills improve with practice and experience. Particularly if you are new to appraisal, it is good to consult other people about appraisal policies and decisions.

Appraisal guidelines

There are some broad guidelines to follow when appraising records for archival value. They essentially act as a set of principles which ensure that appraisal decisions are consistent over time and regardless of the individuals doing it. Figure 4.2 gives principles mapped to guidelines based loosely on the appraisal work of Library and Archives Canada.[1]

1. Preserve records which:

- can be relied on to be accurate and genuine, created by the entity in the course of business or social activity
- are master records, unique to the organization/individual(s)
- complement or supplement other records
- document over time the key goals, decisions, policies and actions of the organization according to its mission statement
- demonstrate origins of the organization/individual(s), their legal status, and structure over time
- provide evidence of key events, projects, programmes, activities and decisions
- document the impact of the organization/individual(s) in the personal, social, economic or political arena
- protect individual and collective rights
- document the birth, background, professional status and significant life events of the individual.

2. Look for:

- record series and groups that are complete and comprehensive
- information-rich summary records.

3. Remember:

- if the series is voluminous it is less likely to be archival
- the requirements of current and future stakeholders to study, assess and understand the work and impact of the creating body
- you may need to select information providing significant context and background to the archives which is not unique and archival.

Figure 4.2 *Appraisal guidelines*

It should be noted that archives have two kinds of value: they document the history of the entity (evidential value); they also contain data which, especially when combined with external sources, provide important resources for research and discovery in other fields (informational value). For example, a series of press cuttings from the Selfridges archives primarily shows that the store advertised widely and was often the subject of newspaper articles. It also provides an insight into social history, as it provides illustrations and commentary on, for example, fashion and home furnishings.

These guidelines can be tailored to your own organization but in any case will need to be periodically reviewed in the same way as retention schedules because functions and activities of individuals and organizations change, but also because the goals of the archive repository might change as well.

Appraisal methods

Chapter 3 discusses the concept of functional appraisal and analysing what the organization does in order to assign retention value to the record series. Archival appraisal, or deciding whether to keep records for the archives because of their historical value, also works at series level. This is because we are assessing the importance of the activity that engenders the records. If the activity is a key one for the organization, then the records are more likely to be archival. For example, the Milson Widget Company board deliberations clearly determine the policy and actions of an organization, so the minutes of board meetings recording board decisions are archival. The Widget Catalogue, brought out twice a year by Marketing and Sales, shows the range of different widgets manufactured over time and is also archival. The invoices sent out to customers are not archival because the annual accounts will show the overall financial picture of the company.

In practice there are several approaches to appraising records:

- micro-appraisal: examining the individual records in some detail to gain an understanding of the content and importance of the decisions and activities documented ('bottom-up')
- macro-appraisal: researching the overall functions and work of the organization to identify the organizational unit with chief responsibility for key activities the repository seeks to document ('top-down')
- a combination of the macro- and micro-appraisal.

Micro-appraisal is most useful when appraising older records where there is no longer a connection with the creators or the archivist is unfamiliar with the creating body and its records. Macro-appraisal has been extremely effective in large organizations (such as the Canadian government) where the sheer volume of records required a more broad-brush approach. Combining the two methods is a good option, because it is only by examining the records we can be sure they actually document the story of the organization, whilst if we do not have the overall picture of all records arising from the various activities and functions, we cannot ensure that there are no gaps or duplications.

Appraisal in action

Appraisal also needs to be carried out in the context of the collecting policy, and can be seen as a four-part exercise, as follows:

1 The collecting policy dictates the subject-matter or content of the archives. It tells us what kinds of organizations are likely to have

archives that we want for our repository.

2 Appraisal is brought to bear to establish which specific record series will be kept permanently as the historical record.
3 Some of the records may need to be weeded if their content includes non-archival material.
4 Bulky record series which cannot be kept in their entirety because of resource constraints can be sampled to ensure that some evidence of the activity survives.

For a concrete example of how it works, let's take a (fictional) archive repository called the London Theatre Archives. Its remit is to collect and make available the archives of theatres in central London. It is offered the records of the Ealing Theatre Company but refers the donor to the London Borough of Ealing Local History Centre because the theatre does not fall in its geographic boundaries. It does however take the Somers Town Community Theatre (STCT) records, as the theatre is situated in central London. The records, when they arrive, turn out to be all records older than five years, regardless of their historical value, so the London Theatre Archives appraisal guidelines are used to identify the main archival series. Everything else is destroyed, in line with the acquisition agreement, except some financial records which need to be retained for six years – these are returned to the theatre manager. One of the record series 'performance records' includes a file for every performance which contains at least one example of all of the publications printed, such as programmes, posters, tickets and sometimes even t-shirts and other merchandise. It was decided to weed the files down to a specified set of documentation (large format poster, small format programme, newspaper advert) and destroy all other records. The t-shirts were photographed if the design differed from the posters and returned to the theatre. This ensured that STCT's core publicity records were retained. Another record series is actor files, one for every actor that trod the boards of STCT. These files are full of information about the actors' (and actresses') amateur dramatic or professional acting careers and background, and include photographs as well as a form which gives the STCT performance(s) they appeared in, a brief profile of the individual and even press cuttings. It is an exceedingly large series and because of space constraints it is decided that the series must be sampled by keeping every tenth file, ensuring that a cross-section is kept to give an indication of the actors and their backgrounds.

Arrangement and description

Archival arrangement and description: the process of mapping, analysing and documenting archival records to produce a finding aid that supports access, preservation and other management activity.

It is difficult to separate arrangement from description, since without arrangement the description cannot begin, and on the other hand the purpose of arranging, or mapping out the relationships between records in a single archive, is to document it and preserve the original order. In Chapter 1 we introduced some key concepts for managing archives. We defined archives as 'records of one organization, family or individual' and secondly noted that the creator (individual, family or organization) is also known as the 'provenance'. Thirdly, we discussed the principle of original order of records 'as they were when last used' by the creator. These concepts will be seen in action in this section, which explains how we come to understand the archival records and document their relationships and content so as to explain them for others, be they researchers or colleagues. Finally, it is important to note the difference between physical control, which seeks to manage the location and condition of archives, and intellectual control, which is about knowing the content matter.

What is description?

Let's first look at description, what it is, what it aims to do and who benefits from it. Description is a term that people working in archives use for the main finding aid that they create to support access to and management of each individual archive in the repository. Obviously *en masse* the descriptions provide a powerful global management tool, but we will focus on description for archives from one provenance. Description is also sometimes referred to as cataloguing, which implies a fairly simple listing and does not cover the complexity of description work and the resulting finding aid.

Description documents the archive in detail, showing the relationship between the different record series and the links between the individual records in each series. As has been said earlier, it provides a written map of the records as created by the organization. It also provides context by documenting the creator, both the overall provenance, but also the subordinate organizational units (or family members) who created individual record groups and series.

Record group: set of record series created by the same organizational unit.

The purpose of description is not simply to support researchers in accessing the contents of the archives, although this is a very important aspect of the work. It also allows the contents of the archives to be identified and located and provides an invaluable tool for archive staff to use in managing the archive, including stocktaking, security and space management. It supports preservation management, particularly in preventing unnecessary handling (and wear and tear) of originals due to finding aids that are not detailed enough.

We can see from this that description benefits many different stakeholders, but the main ones are the archive creators and owners, repository staff and researchers.

What is arrangement?

Archival arrangement is not sorting or classifying the records in the archive into what seems to be a logical or useful order; it is identifying the original order of the records when they were actively used and managed by the creators. This identification process can require painstaking research. The reason we do it before we attempt to document the archive is because it is the best way of retaining all of the evidential value of the records and maintaining the complete story. If we attempt to classify the individual records according to an external system we not only destroy the context and evidence, but we risk over-complicating the task. A subject-based system, for example, will need to be specially tailored to the content of the archive as well as full of cross-references to accommodate items which cover more than one subject. It is always possible to create an index to the description or even the content of the records at a later date.

How do we arrange archives?

In arranging archives we adhere to the principle of provenance. Provenance, as we know, is the creator of the records. The principle dictates that we do not split the records from one creator and those from different provenances should not be mixed. This means that we do not treat the archives of two different widget factories as one, for example, nor even the records pertaining to the same event or person which have different provenances. It also means we do not put all of the committee minutes together, regardless of which part of the organization created them. Similarly we don't put all of the photographs together in the description, although we might store them together once we have established and properly documented their relationships to other records.

When approaching a new arrangement task, the most important thing is not to move things around without noting where it was physically in relation to the other records. In fact the best attitude is one of research and investigation without being too quick to reorganize anything. Bearing all of this in mind, arrangement is a series of steps, as follows:

1 Review any lists or other finding aids that came with the records.

2 Use annual reports, mission statements and organizational charts, if available, to learn about the work and structure of the organization.
3 Carefully examine all of the records in their containers as they came to you, referring to any notes that may have been made prior to their move.
4 Identify the series and their creating organizational units.
5 Document the organizational units as they fit into the organization's hierarchy and assign the record series to the correct creating units.

Having done this, you should end up with a list of record series and their creating units which will allow you to put the series into a hierarchy. Figure 4.3 shows a partial list of the series identified during the arrangement of the archives of Milson Widget Company. Notice that this is also a good time to do some appraisal work.

BOARD MINUTES 1956-2010 11 bound volumes master = ARCHIVAL
BOARD MINUTES 1985-2003 loose papers, ex Head of Prod. Support COPIES - keep as spare
BOARD MINUTES 1999-2007 digital (not viewed) ex H of Prod Del. DELETE
REPORTS TO BOARD 1995-2010 16 files all bound into minute volumes - keep as spare
PRODUCT DEV^T MONTHLY REPORTS 1990-2010 ARCHIVAL not all go to Board & contain key prod. dev't info
PRODUCT SUPPORT MONTHLY REPORTS 1980-2010 DESTROY - routine
REPORTS TO DIVISION HEADS (6 series) DESTROY general management stuff

Figure 4.3 *Arrangement of the MWC Ltd archives: rough series list*

We saw the organizational chart for MWC in Chapter 3. This can be used with the list of series to work out the arrangement scheme shown in Figure 4.4 for the board and the Product Delivery Division.

We now have the hierarchical structure for the description, as shown in Figure 4.5 for MWC's Board and Product Delivery Division records.

Artificial arrangements

Sometimes you will find archival material that is very disorganized, because it has been moved around a lot, or the records were never well managed when they were current, or even perhaps reorganized by someone who did not understand the principles of archives and records management. If you really cannot be sure of the original order, then you will need to put it into some kind of order and the best way to do it is to try to identify the work that gave rise to the records. Thus, for example, the staff records would belong together, the financial ones form a different record group and the operational records a third one. It may be that your hierarchy would be quite flat because you

Organizational unit	Record series
1 MWC board	• Board minutes 1956–2010 (11 bound volumes) • Board correspondence 1965–2010 (4 bound volumes, 5 ring binders) • Annual Report and Accounts 1956–2010 (55 slim publications)
1.1 Product Delivery Division	• Monthly reports 1990–2010 (21 files)
1.1.1 Development	• Development plans 1950s, 1979–2010 (4 bundles) • Development projects 1985–2010 (circa 50 files, includes research) • Development Unit Research files 1980s–2010 (weed to retain significant research that did not lead to a project)
1.1.2 Production	• Annual production plan 1975–2010 (7 files) • New parts acquisition 1993–2010 (2 files) • Production statistics 1962–2010 (1 ring binder)
1.1.3 Marketing and Sales	• Widget catalogues 1956–2010 (55 slim publications) • Press cuttings and adverts 1970–2010 (41 comb-bound volumes) • Mail-outs 1970–2010 (select for archives)
Reference copies	• Board minutes 1985–2003 (loose papers) • Product Support: Reports to Board 1995–2007 (16 files)
Destroy/delete	• Product Development: Board minutes 1999–2007 (digital) • Product Support: monthly reports (routine admin) • Division management team meetings (routine admin) • Unit reports to Division Heads (routine admin) • Development: Competitor files • Production: Maintenance schedule 2005–2008 • Marketing: Advertising accounts
Scheduled for destruction	• Production's Maintenance schedule 2009–2010 (routine). Destroy January 2016 and 2017

Figure 4.4 *Arrangement scheme for part of MWC Ltd's archives*

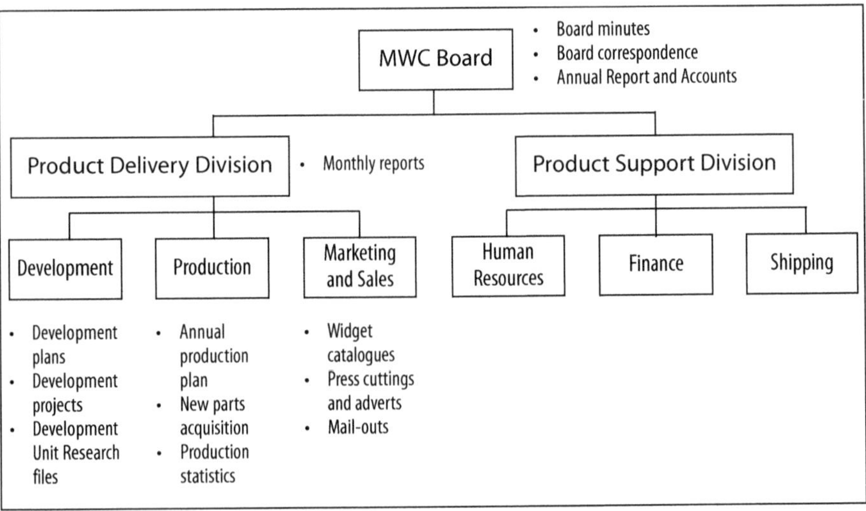

Figure 4.5 *Structure of arrangement scheme for part of MWC Ltd's archives*

have no idea of what the organizational chart looked like.

Whether the arrangement you use is one that was obvious from the way you found the records in the filing cabinets, or you have had to painstakingly reconstruct it as best you could or impose one on hopelessly messed up records, you should document what you have done. Explain what you did and why, so that if more information turned up in future, any necessary adjustments could be made.

Describing archives

Our definition of arrangement and description includes 'documenting archival records to produce a finding aid' and, as we also said earlier, description is the term we use for the main finding aid which documents the records in context according to the way they were created and last used. Thus, description does two things: it maps out the arrangement of the records and describes the content, context and characteristics. As we already know from the arrangement section, the records will probably be in a hierarchy, with items at the bottom, through record series and record groups, to the provenance level at the top. The description needs to reflect and document this, as well as capture the elements necessary for good, accurate description. This means that archival description can be a complex, hierarchical construct with different description elements at different levels in the hierarchy, although in practice it is usual to have the contextual and cumulative information at the top (provenance) level, more specific contextual information at the record group level and the detailed description of the records and their content at the series level.

What to include in description

We are fortunate that we have an internationally recognized standard which guides us in deciding the information elements we need in our description. The standard, produced by the International Council on Archives, is called the *International Standard on Archival Description* (General) (ISAD(G) for short). There is also a related standard, the *International Standard Archival Authority Record for Corporate Bodies, Persons and Families* (ISAAR CPF), which gives a checklist of information elements for documenting record creators. Together these two international standards[2] provide a simple metadata checklist. Table 4.2 gives the list and explanations where necessary.

You will not need to include all of this information at every level in your hierarchical description. In fact it is a principle of the international descriptive standard that you do not repeat information, but rather include it higher up. Thus the organization's administrative history will only be needed at the top,

Table 4.2 *ISAD(G) and ISAAR(CPF) description elements*

Area	Element	Notes	Reference
Identity: unique identifier; documents overall size and content	Reference code*	A unique reference	ISAD(G) 1.1
	Title*	Short, obvious name for the archive	ISAD(G) 1.2
	Date(s)*	Covering dates	ISAD(G) 1.3
	Level of description*	e.g., series, item	ISAD(G) 1.4
	Extent and medium*	Amount and format	ISAD(G) 1.5
Context: provenance; history of the records	Name of creator(s)*	**Authorized form of name,*** or various names used by or for the creator over time	ISAD(G) 2.1 ISAAR 5.1
	Administrative/biographical history	**Type*** of creating organization, family or person, **dates of existence,*** history, places of operation, legal status, significant relationships, etc.	ISAD(G) 2.2 ISAAR 5.1, 5.2 and 5.3
	Archival history	Places and custody	ISAD(G) 2.3
	Immediate source of acquisition or transfer	Person, organization or vendor	ISAD(G) 2.4
Content and structure: details content; arrangement; where these archives fit in overall record landscape of creator(s)	Scope and content	The detailed description of the records	ISAD(G) 3.1
	Appraisal, destruction and scheduling information	Details of any appraisal that has been carried out, either before or after transfer	ISAD(G) 3.2
	Accruals	If the creator is still producing records, there may be more to come	ISAD(G)3.3
	System of arrangement	Notes on original order and/or arrangement of the records	ISAD(G) 3.4

*mandatory

Continued on facing page

or fonds, level, whereas specific detail about the work which resulted in the ground-breaking discovery of widget IB2002 would belong in the description of the research project files.

Style and format

Archival description comes in a myriad of different styles and formats. It is usual to at least create description as a digital record which can easily be corrected, updated and used for basic searching. A number of software packages are available, both proprietary and open source, commercial and free. These allow more sophisticated searching and reporting on descriptive information – but also can have functionality to allow for more global management of the archives, for example including location and access

Table 4.2 *Continued*

Area	Element	Notes	Reference
Access and use: conditions and requirements for access	Conditions governing access		ISAD(G) 4.1
	Conditions governing reproduction		ISAD(G) 4.2
	Language/scripts of material		ISAD(G) 4.3
	Physical characteristics, technical requirements	Preservation issues, software or hardware required to read records	ISAD(G) 4.4
	Finding aids	Other finding aids	ISAD(G) 4.5
Related materials: details of copies; other records from same provenance not included in material being documented	Existence and location of originals		ISAD(G) 5.1
	Existence and location of copies		ISAD(G) 5.2
	Related units of description		ISAD(G) 5.3
	Publication note	Any publications based on the material	ISAD(G) 5.4
Notes:	Note	Any information that does not fit into the other categories	ISAD(G) 6.1
Control:	Archivist's note	Account of how the description was done, research resources	ISAD(G) 7.1
	Rules or conventions	Any standards or in-house rules followed in writing the description	ISAD(G) 7.2
	Date(s) of descriptions	Name of archivist	ISAD(G) 7.3
			* mandatory

information. Some of them comply with the standards but regardless of whether the software is configured to in-house rules, standards or both, automated systems do help to ensure that everyone doing description work does it consistently over time.

What ISAD(G) calls 'scope and content' is the meat of the description. This may be written in note form, in bullets or in proper text with sentences and paragraphs. When writing description, bear in mind you are aiming to give the researcher a clear representation of what the records are about. The amount of detail you write will depend on the time available, but will also be in harmony with that of other description both within the fonds and across the repository. Try to write objectively, concisely and accurately – and look at some of the excellent archival description that has been published on line.

Publishing and using description documentation

When you have completed your description, it is a good idea to have someone read it over to ensure that it is as clear and objective as you would like it to be. Once you are satisfied it is ready, you can make it available, either in the reading room in hard copy, or visible in your cataloguing software or on line.

There is another standard that it is important to know about, called Encoded Archival Description. It is a way to code description documentation published on the internet in such a way that your description documentation can be searched in a structured way, along with other coded description. So, to give a simple search example, if a researcher is interested in widget development in English-speaking countries, they could search on 'widget' via one of the archival description networks and, because the scope and content fields have been tagged as such, all of the archives with 'widget' in their description would be found.

If you aim to record at least the mandatory elements in your accession record, and aim to include as many as possible of the rest of them in your description work, you can be sure that you have written a good piece of archival description, your researchers will know what the records will contain and you will be in a position to publish and share your description in any of the major online description networks, provided you do the necessary technical tagging.

Finding aids

> **Finding aids:** documentation about the archives which helps to identify, locate and manage them.

In Chapter 1 we learned that finding aids play an important role in managing and accessing archival material. In the previous section we learned that the most important finding aid is archival description, which documents the archives in their original order and is the result of a careful work process. We also mentioned the existing finding aids which come with the records, so we know that there are a number of different types of finding aid. There are several reasons for this. One is that when they were current, the records needed a classification scheme or a file list to help the creators and users file and retrieve records. Another reason is to allow users (and archivists) to search across different archival fonds for content relevant to specific lines of research. Even within one archival fonds it is useful to search the content and one way of doing that is to compile an index. Whilst the description may be seen as the map of the archive, as with many maps, it is useful to have a street or landmark index. Archive users, particularly first-time researchers, will be expecting indexes to help them locate the material that interests them. Thus indexes can be invaluable not just in helping to find specific archival material, but also in terms of helping our researchers navigate through and use our finding aids effectively.

Finding aids for word searches

Indexes, keyword lists, thesauri and naming rules all play a role in assisting word searches. Originally it was an effective way of providing points of entry to archival content in the pre-computer era, and now it is a way of providing a faster more focused alternative to full text retrieval.

There are two main kinds of indexes for archives. The first is an index of the archival description documentation, which involves selecting and alphabetizing reference terms, such as personal names, place names and subjects, from the description document. The other is an index of the content of the records themselves. This latter kind of indexing is often done by volunteers with a specific interest in the records. For example, the local genealogical society might volunteer to index the names in parish registers. It is particularly useful to index record groups which have been demonstrated to be heavily used over time – it allows researchers to more accurately pin-point the exact records they are interested in (or saves a fruitless inspection of the records) but it also reduces wear and tear on the archives.

Keyword lists identify significant words and for archival finding aids this usually means people, places and subjects which are well represented in the holdings. For example, an archive repository specializing in records of women's history might develop a keyword list of language around, for example, women's suffrage or key individuals, events and places in the movement. The keyword list can then act as a way to tag finding aids and archival content. It means that those tagging the archives and those searching the archives have a common vocabulary. Keyword lists can be used as drop-down menus in archival description software, which is a great way to ensure that everyone inputting description uses consistent terms. Archivists, like librarians, also use thesauri to guide the use of vocabulary both in the archival description and in indexing terms. It is probably true to say, however, that a keyword list is usually sufficient to ensure that the language used is consistent and supports effective retrieval.

The use of naming conventions, or rules, can be crucial to ensuring that it is quick and easy to search finding aids for specific research interests. Let's take the example of an individual called Henry Alexander St John Smith, who is called Harry by his family and close friends. He was born into a noble family and as the eldest son had the title Earl Smith from birth but on his father's death inherited a dukedom and subsequently became the Duke of Mornshire. The family and estate papers refer to him variously as Harry,

Earl Smith, the 5th Duke and HASJ Smith – and there are other family members with similar names. A naming convention could be established for the Mornshire Archive which helps to clarify and distinguish between the various family members, as well as help the archivist decide what form of the name to consistently use. Similarly, a naming convention which encompassed a range of different archival fonds in a single repository could also be used to guide cataloguers, indexers and researchers in consistent forms of names to speed up searches. Other examples where guidance is needed include organizational units (especially when there is reorganization and/or names change) and whether to use acronyms or extend them fully.

Other types of finding aids

One really important finding aid, which we usually do not share with our researchers, is the location register. Location registers list the archive material, usually by reference number or name, and its location in the storage area. A computerized location register will allow searching, so the order does not particularly matter, but it is also sensible to have a print-out available in the storage area for reference, especially if the computer is unavailable for any reason. Apart from this, the description itself and any indexes, other finding aids may be necessary. Table 4.3 gives a list of these.

Automated finding aids

Use of technology in developing archival description and finding aids can cut out unnecessary duplication of information and effort as well as ensure that the result is user-friendly and allows quick retrieval for researchers and archive staff alike. However, it is important to consider the options – and goals – carefully before embarking on implementing new technology. Remember that a simple word-processed document may be good enough to allow you to provide access to the archives and manage their use and preservation.

Automation and digitization

This section discusses how to use computers to manage archival records in all media. It also addresses automating legacies of paper-based archival finding aids. Modern computer technology has revolutionized archives and records management work. The benefits of using it well include:

- the removal of a lot of the repetition and duplication of work necessary with manual systems (for example creating many index cards for one archival catalogue)

Table 4.3 *Archive finding aids*

Finding aid	**Description**	**Example**	**Author**
Description	Documents records in order into which organized by creator	Catalogue of the records of the Milson Widget Company	Trained archive staff
Location register	List of all archive fonds in repository	Location guide for holdings of MWC	Trained archive staff
Index	Alphabetized list of people, places, names, etc., which feature in the description and/or the archive material; gives information about archival content	Hand- and typewritten card catalogues of subjects, place and personal names from the MWC archives description	Trained archive staff; record creators; volunteers
Classification scheme	Hierarchical list of record categories	Classification scheme for MWC Development Unit project files	Record creators
File list	List of individual files in file series	List of the MWC sales catalogues	Trained archive staff; record creators; volunteers
Repository guide	List of all the archival finds in the repository, sometimes classified according to type of organization (e.g., public, business, personal papers)	Guide to the holdings of the County Archives	Trained archive staff
Theme/subject guides	List of all the records in the repository that are useful for particular kinds of research	Guide to researching the history of buildings in the County Archives	Trained archive staff; volunteers
Box list	List giving brief summary of content of boxes, usually as preliminary to appraisal or description work	List of contents of accession ref 2015/005 accrual to records of the Milson Widget Company	Trained archive staff; record creators; volunteers
Shelf list	List giving details of what is on shelves – can be box numbers and references or items, depending on how organized the holdings are	Shelf list for Strong Room B	Trained archive staff; volunteers
Guide to records in more than one repository	List giving summary details about holdings of archives in a geographic region or with similar collecting policies	A Guide to Scottish Audiovisual Archives	Trained archive staff; volunteers; commissioned researchers

- increased consistency across people and over time
- the publication of archival description relatively cheaply on the internet, allowing potential researchers and other stakeholders to be well informed about the holdings without needing to visit the repository
- digitization of archives saving researchers time and travel expense, as well as saving wear and tear on the archives.

In order to benefit from the technology, we need to understand not only our own archives management goals, but also what the technology can actually do. We need to weigh up the costs together with the pros and cons of designing an in-house solution in contrast to buying something off the shelf. Above all, it is important to understand, as with all IT projects, that the technology can only be as successful as the human input – the work flows, metadata schemas and reporting requirements must be identified, analysed and mapped out to ensure that the requirements are clear. From this preliminary work it is possible to develop a functional specification which can be used either to design an in-house solution or to assess off-the-shelf software. Automation projects require a lot of work up front to ensure that the solution is fit for purpose. The archival description and other information about the archives need to be organized. Rules and conventions which meet the prevailing standards also need to be incorporated into the software structure. Finally, remember that you will almost certainly need to have good technical support, if there is no one on your team who has skills and experience in specifying, installing and implementing common or specialized software.

Functional specifications

Functional specification: detailed list of tasks or processes required of an automated system in order to meet operational needs.

Regardless of whether you are automating your archive management processes for the first time or upgrading an existing automated system, it is important to be clear about what the software needs to do. This will form the basis of your functional specification which lists system requirements. Initially it is useful to map out the repository functions and activities together with existing documentation on the holdings before fleshing out the requirements in more detail. Table 4.4 gives a list of functions mapped to existing documentation and required functionality.

Note how the documentation is relevant to more than one area of archives management; for example, the location register is important to access, space management and preservation activity. Similarly, the necessary functionality crosses documentation (or data, once it is in the system) and functions, as with the requirement to be able to publish information on the internet.

In writing your specification, take into consideration the international archival description standards, in particular ISAD(G) and ISAAR mentioned in 'What to include in description' above. You will also need to bear in mind copyright requirements, Freedom of Information legislation and protecting personal data. The standards and legal requirements have an impact on working practices and it is useful to check the functional specification against them to ensure compliance.

The detailed specification list should focus on what you need the

Table 4.4 *Archival management functions, documentation and software functionality*

Archival function	Existing documentation	Functionality
Accessioning	• accession register	• data entry of key information about material • details of depositors
Appraisal	• appraisal guidelines • retention schedules	• mapping to collecting policy • documenting appraisal decisions
Description	• organizational history; biography • series descriptions • file and volume lists	• data entry of detailed information about content and context at multiple levels • publication of description on internet
Space management	• location register	• registering location of records • logging movement of records
Creating finding aids	• guides • leaflets	• manipulation of data to produce indexes, lists, information papers and other publications • publication of finding aids on internet
Preservation management	• conservation survey • production records	• tagging and prioritizing records for conservation • documenting preservation/conservation work • managing preservation copying programs • limiting access to fragile documents • flagging up high-use documents
Access management	• production forms • location register • website	• data searches • checking records out and in • logging researcher information • security tagging of records • logging use of records • management of reference enquiries • publicize services on internet
Outreach	• publications • exhibition records • website	• data searches • adding publication and exhibition notes • publicize services on internet

technology to do, not how it could be done. One of the benefits of automating archival management is that it can reveal different and potentially better ways of doing things. By not stipulating how the new system should do something, more options will be revealed. Similarly, an automation project is an opportunity to review all of your archive management work processes, so make the scope of your specification as wide as possible, listing everything, no matter how basic or trivial.

Once you have mapped out all of the required functionality, you will need to check that it is clearly expressed. It is better to write in unabbreviated language and describe in detail what is needed so that the requirement is unambiguous – vendors and IT professionals will not be familiar with our professional jargon and shorthand. Thus 'Provide search functionality across all descriptive data in the holdings, in a variety of ways, including but not limited to, keyword searches, free text searches, searches on specific fields' is better than 'Allow searching by keyword, free text and specific fields'. It is also good to assign a performance value to a function, such as stipulating that a search must take no longer than one minute.

Part of a functional specification for the access module of an automated archives management system might look like that in Figure 4.6. Notice that this example differentiates between essential requirements, expressed as 'must', and requirements that are desirable, expressed as 'may'. It is important for the specification to be graded, particularly if you have chosen a very broad spectrum. Decide which functionality is crucial to help eliminate systems that are unfit for purpose.

The system **must**:

- provide search functionality across all descriptive data in the holdings, in a variety of ways including but not limited to keyword searches, free text searches, searches on specific fields
- permit the configuration of forms and reports, both as fixed templates for re-use and ad hoc
- create and track information about movement of records before and after use, together with details of individuals handing them.

The system **may**:

- allow sensitive and closed records to be tagged and controlled.

Figure 4.6 *Example of part of a functional specification*

As archives professionals we will tend to organize our functional specification document according to the different aspects of managing archives. However, many of the functional requirements we assign to one work area will equally apply to others, as we already noted. The ability to search the content of the system is probably necessary for all work, but not all of the work will require the full range of search functionality. Data capture and inputting functionality is another example of this.

Technical specifications must also be included. These pertain to the technical infrastructure and the general requirements of the automation project. Examples of technical requirements might be that the system works in both a Windows and a Mac environment or that the system is compatible with cloud storage and remote access. It is in this area that we need to work most closely with the IT specialists.

Regardless of whether you are in the market for an off-the-shelf archives management package, using open-source freeware such as ICA's AtoM,[3] or you are customizing common office software such as an MS Access database, your completed set of functional requirements will really help. You can use it in the following ways:

- to review your existing software package to identify the gaps to make the case for upgrading the technology
- to make it part of your tender documentation for software vendors
- to turn it into a checklist to support assessment of off-the-shelf software
- to make sure that you use all of the functionality you need in your AtoM solution
- to use it to identify requirements for your customized Access database.

Finally, it is worth taking a moment to consider joining up the separate (potential) technological components that can be used to support the management of archives. You may be in a position to commission a piece of kit that will do it all, but if not you may want to make sure they all play nicely together. Figure 4.7 illustrates some of the possible components, with the archives management package (AMP) at the centre. The metadata from the digital archive should feed into the AMP to allow searching across all media, whilst some of the digital archive's metadata will have been captured with the records from the ERMS. Similarly, the copies in the digital image library will be of originals in the digital archives, and the metadata can be shared. With the website, the copies may have come from either the digital archive or the image library, but the website itself may be captured as snapshots and taken into the digital archive.

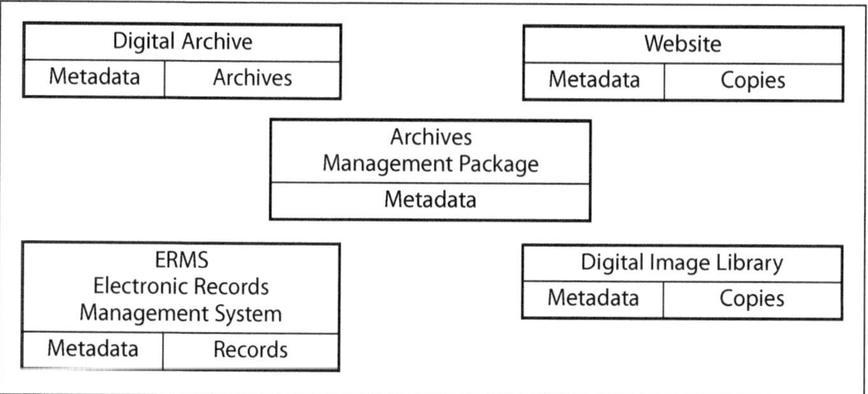

Figure 4.7 *Archives management package components*

Digitization projects

There is sometimes confusion about the role of digitization in archives management, as well as misconceptions as to its potential to save money. Digitization of archives means creating a digital image of a physical record. This could be a text-based record, such as a baptism register, or a visual record, such as a photograph. We digitize archives for several reasons:

- to create a surrogate for researchers to access remotely
- to prevent more wear and tear on heavily used or fragile records
- to change them into a format that enables them to be aggregated with other records and used in different ways, for example using optical character recognition to index the content
- to have a readily accessible copy of the record if the original needs to be stored remotely
- to use in exhibitions or publications.

As an archives management tool, digitization technology is invaluable but it also comes at a price and the digital image can never totally replace the original. Prior to undertaking a digitization project it is important to conduct a thorough feasibility study and to understand the pros and cons, as well as what it will entail. The key to successful digitization projects is quality control, which is very challenging, given that the act of creating a digital image from original archive material is inherently boring. It involves:

- capturing the image using a scanning machine or camera
- checking that the image is clear
- changing the capture format as necessary to allow for access and preservation copies as required
- ensuring the image has a meaningful name and adding metadata as required.

Quality control, another important but potentially boring task, needs to be built in to the process – by a different person. Thus the initial work is labour-intensive and has a cost implication.

Once the images have been created, together with their descriptive and management metadata, they need to be stored in a repository. Whilst the metadata may give enough information either to link images which together represent a whole record or to link related records, the repository might also usefully have a folder structure to make this easier. The repository and its contents will need to be subject to a digital preservation strategy, as outlined in Chapter 5 of this book. This is potentially risky and definitely costly over time, so the benefits need to be weighed against the costs.

Access

Access: providing colleagues, selected audiences or the wider public with facilities to consult archives, including provision of finding aids and advice

As we mentioned in Chapter 1, we keep archives so that people can consult and use them. However, this aim goes beyond the needs of contemporary citizens, researchers and colleagues – we intend that people in the future will also be able to access and use them. It can be hard to balance the interests of the public, politicians and management with our own responsibility to ensure that the archives are held in the best possible environment so that they are preserved for future generations. Similarly, the need to describe the archives in context according to the way in which they were created and used does not necessarily result in the most intuitive of finding aids. Managing archives well includes a thoughtful approach to providing access to archives which is appropriate to the aims and funding model of the organization.

Access policy

The foundation of archives access is having a clear policy about who will be given access and under what conditions. Archives funded with public money are usually expected to provide access to the public, particularly their own taxpayers. The Council of Europe's recommendation on a European policy on access to archives[4] states that 'access to public archives is a right. In a political system which respects democratic values, this right should apply to all users regardless of their nationality, status or function.' For private archive repositories the question of who is allowed to access the archives is at the discretion of the organizational decision-makers, which might mean they are totally closed to external researchers. Table 4.5 gives the components of an archives access policy and example text.

The International Council on Archives 'Principles of Access to Archives'[5] also provides a good basis for an access policy.

On-site access

Once an access policy has been established, we need to think how to provide on-site access in such a way that ensures that the archives are handled as little and as carefully as possible at the same time as helping our researchers to understand and use them.

The reading room

Unlike most library holdings, archive material cannot be kept on open shelves for users to browse and help themselves to whatever they fancy. We know the reasons for this already: archives are unique and if they are damaged or lost we cannot replace them; they need to be stored in an environment that will ensure that they are preserved and legible for generations to come;

Table 4.5 *Components of an archives access policy*

Statement area	Example
Mission statement	Archives are kept to preserve the documentary heritage of the Milson Widget Company.
Who can access them	They are available for consultation by anyone upon written application.
Whether enquiries about the content of the archives are handled	The Archivist also accepts enquiries by telephone, letter and e-mail, but the Archivist cannot carry out extended research for those unable to visit in person.
Whether copies of archive material can be supplied	Requests for copies of archival material may also be granted at a small charge and subject to copyright provisions.
Promotion of the archives	The Milson Widget Company is committed to raising awareness of the content of its archives, making finding aids available on the website and working with other repositories and heritage organizations to promote the history of the widget industry in the UK and overseas.
Provision for disabled users	The archives consultation room is not easily accessible to those with mobility issues, but provision can be made for users on the ground floor subject to 5 days' notice.
Priority user groups	The Milson Widget Company particularly welcomes enquiries and access requests from Milson's employees and their families.
Opening hours	The archives may be consulted during normal office hours by appointment.
Access conditions	Access is provided in the archives consultation room on the 3rd floor of the Milson's headquarters building under the supervision of a member of the archives team. Users are expected to follow the access guidelines. Access to certain records may be refused where the privacy of individuals, commercial confidentiality of Milson or legislation may be contravened, similarly if the records are too fragile to be handled.

archives are not managed in ways to support physical browsing. Therefore, providing access to the archives requires special provision and resources.

Most importantly, there needs to be a space where staff can sit with researchers consulting the archives. Ideally this would be a dedicated reading room, but in an organizational archive or low-resource environment it may have to be the archivist's office. The reading room needs to have a desk for the supervising staff and tables (and chairs) for researchers, one of the tables may need to be big if the holdings include large-format maps and plans. The lighting needs to be good enough to read by, but set up so that the heat and light levels are not harmful to the archives. Window glass needs to filter out ultra-violet rays and direct sunlight should not fall on surfaces where the archives are. Ideally the reading room will be accessible to people with mobility difficulties and at least one of the tables should have adjustable height to accommodate wheelchairs. It is good to have a table, trolley or shelves to hold archive material awaiting consultation or return to the strong room. All the finding aids should be available too, either hard copy or digital via a computer terminal set up for researchers to use. Obviously, in a highly automated environment record requests could be made through this terminal too. Another crucial aspect of reading room management is the procedure for researchers to order archives. The tried and trusted way in the manual environment is a tripartite carbon copy form. One copy is placed on the shelf or in the box to facilitate correct replacement after use. One copy stays with the item to ensure that it gets to the right researcher and can be easily returned afterwards. The third copy stays with the reading room staff as a control – all three slips should be married up at the end of the day to ensure that all the archives have been returned to storage.

> **Production:** the process of locating, fetching and giving archives to researchers for consultation whilst tracking them.

Apart from these basic necessities, and depending on the archive formats, the following equipment and facilities are useful:

- book rests, document supports
- weights
- magnifying glasses
- light box
- ultra-violet light
- reference collection
- equipment to view digital and audiovisual archives
- microfilm/fiche viewers
- pencils.

You also need to think about provision for bags and coats, which researchers cannot keep with them, as well as toilet facilities and places for people to eat. Large archive repositories may have catering facilities or a lunch room on site, but for low-resource operations a list of local cafés and restaurants may be a good solution.

Reading room guidelines

The most important thing to impress on researchers is the importance of preventing damage to the records – we do this through a set of rules or guidelines which set out the conditions of use. Table 4.6 gives a list of guidelines together with an indication of why each one is necessary.

Customer care

Chapter 1 discusses the various types of archive users and their perspectives, giving us an idea of the wide spectrum of age, education and expectation with

Table 4.6 *Reading room guidelines*

Rule	Reason
The archives may only be consulted in the reading room.	Archives are unique therefore they cannot be lent out or used without supervision.
Coats, bags and personal belongings (except writing materials, laptops or tablets, mobile phones and purses) must be left in the lockers provided.	Records can be hidden in bags and coats: if coats are damp the humidity levels in the reading room will rise.
All researchers are requested to provide contact information, demographic data and details of their research interests and to sign in when visiting the archives. These are kept in accordance with privacy legislation.	To ensure the security of the archives, assist individuals' research enquiries and to gather statistics on archive use.
Archive material must be handled carefully at all times, in accordance with the handling guidelines. Archives staff can also provide advice.	To prevent physical harm to the archives.
Pencil only may be used, no ink.	Ink cannot be easily removed from archive material.
No food or drink may be brought into the reading room or consumed whilst consulting the archives.	Food and drink attracts insects and other pests and can spill on the archives.
Please respect the needs of other researchers and keep noise to a minimum: mobile phones must be set to silent.	The reading room needs to provide an atmosphere conducive to research.
Researchers may make images of archive records and/or request copies from the archives (for a charge) provided permission is granted according to copyright legislation.	Researchers often need copies of archives but copyright legislation must be respected and the cost of reproduction services may need to be covered.
The reading room is open from 9 a.m. to 5 p.m. Monday, Tuesday, Thursday and Friday, from 1 p.m. to 8 p.m. on Wednesdays and from 9 a.m. to 12.30 p.m. on Saturdays. It is closed on public holidays and during the first two weeks in January for stock-taking.	Researchers need to know opening times; staff need time to fetch records at the beginning of the day and return them at the end.
Archive materials can be requested in advance by phone, in writing or via the website, or on-site using the request form. Please allow between 15 and 30 minutes for requests to be filled. Last orders are 30 minutes before the reading room closes.	To clarify the conditions around ordering and delivering archives to the reading room.
Researchers are permitted a maximum of 1 small box, 3 files or 3 volumes on the desk at one time. Please replace items on the returns trolley.	Too many records on the desk risks damage and also makes theft easier.
Fragile records may not be available for consultation, on the advice of the Head Conservator: whenever possible a surrogate copy will be delivered instead.	To warn users that not all records will be available.
A Duty Archivist and Archives Assistant will be on hand in the reading room at all times to assist researchers.	Archives staff need to be in the reading room not only to help users but also to ensure that the archives are being handled carefully and to deter theft.

which we may be dealing. We also know that archival description is not user-friendly, particularly to people who are new to using archives. It is therefore crucial to have archive staff on hand who know the content of the archives in a general way and who also know how to use the finding aids to follow particular lines of research.

Most importantly, the staff who deal with researchers need to have good training in customer care. The aim of customer care is to ensure that users of our archives receive impartial, professional assistance in using the records. Customer care includes providing information about the holdings and access possibilities and conditions as well as introducing new users to the reading room, using the finding aids, ordering records and following the guidelines for use of archives. The benefit of good customer care is that the researchers get the most value out of their visits at the same time as ensuring that the repository resources are deployed effectively and that the records are protected.

Archive reading rooms can be intimidating places and it is important to provide an environment where users feel comfortable asking questions and have confidence that staff are well informed and can assist them in their research. It is equally important that archives staff feel confident that they know how to help researchers, when a researcher is demanding too much and how to keep calm in the potentially stressful reading room environment. Having said that, helping users research the archives can be one of the most rewarding aspects of archives management and the real key is making sure that the users understand that the rules around access are to protect the archives.

Reproduction services

Many archive users, be they on-site users or long-distance researchers, request copies of archive material. We discussed intellectual property rights earlier in this chapter and above all it is important to ensure that any copying services comply with the prevailing copyright law. This may entail asking requesters to sign undertakings that the copies are for personal use or research and not commercial purposes. Many people consulting archives in the reading room will have cameras or mobile phones and will be able to make their own copies – it can be beneficial to allow this, as it is less work for archives staff and an efficient way to meet a user need. You will need to have a system in place to meet copyright requirements, gather statistics, collect any fees and ensure that there are no preservation threats. If you offer a copying service, there are similar considerations but the most important one is that the act of copying the record does not damage it. It is also a good idea to keep images of items that have been copied, to save copying them again. In addition to request and undertaking forms, there should also be guidance on citing the archives for publication and acknowledgement of the repository and any copyright owners.

Enquiry services

All archives receive enquiries about their holdings and specific content. The access policy guides how much actual research archives staff should do on behalf of a user, but it is usual to provide enough information about the holdings to enable users to ascertain whether the archive is relevant to their research. If research is undertaken on behalf of users, there may be a limit to the time spent and/or a charge for it. Enquiries can obviously come in many ways: e-mail, phone, letter, fax. It is usual to have a minimum response time and it should also be noted that legislation on access to information may be applicable for public archive repositories. Whatever the specific legal requirements and access policy, it is a good idea to keep a record of significant research in case it is needed again for a different enquiry or for the more general management of the archives.

User groups

Academic researchers, people looking into the history of their house or community or genealogists – people pursuing a specific, probably one-off line of research – are the kind of archive users which we have been discussing so far. Groups of individuals with similar research interests, or wanting a more general introduction also use archives. Examples include:

- family history societies
- local history societies
- groups with an interest in the subject matter of some or all of the archives (for example an industry, business or creative industry)
- school groups
- student groups
- life-long learning groups.

It is important for the repository to think through how it provides access for these groups and also whether there are ways in which it can work with the groups to enhance access for other users. With school groups it is probable that the reason for the visit is connected with the school curriculum and there will be access visits of this kind over several years. It is therefore worth working with the teachers to ensure that the materials are relevant and interesting and meet the educational needs. It is also an opportunity to introduce children and adolescents to archives. There are similar benefits to working with university professors and approaching student visits in the same way but there is also an opportunity with students to attract them to more independent archival research and/or volunteering in the archives. Local history, family history and subject-oriented history groups can offer a huge opportunity to archives for gathering more detailed knowledge of the holdings, attracting volunteer input and developing a friends group to advocate the archives repository. It follows therefore that taking the time to talk through the group's needs with the leaders, to research and produce the relevant archive material and to explain the finding aids and general content and goals of the repository is time well spent.

Outreach

Many archive users come to the reading room because they have an information need but we should also be thinking about attracting new and different audiences. This is particularly true for publicly funded archives, which may need to demonstrate their relevance and value to the communities they document and serve, but it is also part of a healthy archives management strategy. Understanding our users and potential users will feed into our collecting policies and appraisal work, as well as challenge us to think of new ways to use and advocate the archives. This in turn will provide justification for resources already spent and evidence to support future spending.

Outreach for archives covers a range of activities which the archives staff can do alone or, if the resources are available, is more effective with help from various professionals outside the archives field. Table 4.7 gives some examples.

Table 4.7 *Archives outreach activities*

Example	Description	External expertise
Website	Vehicle to provide information about the repository and its holdings, including images, finding aids and access conditions	Electronic communications and publishing
Social media strategy	Using social media sites and Twitter feeds to advertise events, celebrate achievements and showcase holdings and to generate comment and feedback	Communications
Newsletter	Regular electronic newsletter giving repository news and event alerts	Design for print and electronic publishing
Exhibition work	In-house and external exhibitions featuring the archive holdings	Advanced conservation and preservation, exhibition design
Publications and leaflets	Glossy books featuring images from the archives, guides to holdings, or archives supporting particular research interests	Research, writing and editing, print and electronic publishing
Presence at history fairs	Running a stall to showcase archive holdings that support research interests such as genealogy, local history, etc.	Marketing
Friends Group	Supporting establishment of group of supporters, working with them to achieve common goals such as fundraising or volunteer schemes	Fundraising
Events	Celebration of International Archives Day	Marketing and communications

Outreach work is about having a vision of the ways in which the archives might be used. It raises awareness about the holdings and ensures that the archives are known about and used to the full extent of their potential. Whatever the size of the repository or its resources, it is vital to have that vision and an internal and/or external outreach strategy to ensure that any outreach you are able to do is focused and effective.

Advocacy

As already noted in Chapter 1, advocacy is crucial to managing archives well. It is about raising awareness of the importance and value of archives, ensuring the resources to look after the archives are in place and getting support to maintain them from politicians, managers and citizens. Advocacy activity ranges from staff every day by default demonstrating professionalism and articulating archives messages through to more resource-intensive focused marketing offensives. As with all aspects of managing archives, spending time analysing advocacy goals and working on a strategy is time well spent. The International Council on Archives has an Advocacy Expert Group and some really useful advocacy tools.

Working with volunteers

Archives have always attracted volunteers and the benefits to the work of a repository in terms of extending the resource should be obvious. However, it is important to ensure that volunteers are properly managed and that the work they do is properly integrated into the work plan in line with operational goals. If volunteers are poorly supervised and left to their own devices it is at best a waste of resources and at worst might harm the archives. There are plenty of resources that provide guidance on managing volunteers in general, as well as archives volunteers, including the Archives and Records Association's *Volunteering in Collections Care: best practice guide 2011*.[6] The key things to remember are:

- There has to be a benefit to the volunteer (work experience, stronger application to get onto a training course, job satisfaction, learning experience).
- Include volunteers in the team as much as possible (it is best to give them tasks to do with other people).
- Supervise and evaluate their performance so they can monitor their improvements and achievements.
- Have a variety of different projects ready that are suitable for volunteers.

Remember managing volunteers is about ensuring that the experience is enjoyable for them and meets any goals they might have whilst furthering the work and aims of the repository.

Round-up

Chapter 4 has covered all aspects of managing archives, from deciding the repository's overall content and focus, through selection and appraisal, arrangement and description, to providing access to researchers. Chapter 5 will cover preservation management, which underpins all other archival work.

Notes

1 www.bac-lac.gc.ca/eng/services/government-information-resources/disposition/records-appraisal-disposition-program/Pages/preserving-archival-historical-memory-government.aspx.
2 www.ica.org/10206/standards/standards-list.html.
3 www.ica-atom.org.
4 https://wcd.coe.int/ViewDoc.jsp?id=362167&Site=COE.
5 www.ica.org/13619/toolkits-guides-manuals-and-guidelines/principles-of-access-to-archives.html.
6 www.archives.org.uk/images/documents/VOLUNTEERING_in_COLLECTIONS_CARE_-_GUIDE-1.pdf.

CHAPTER 5

Archival preservation

Introduction

> **Preservation:** the function of ensuring archives are managed, stored and used under conditions that ensure their longevity.

Preservation is the function which underpins everything we do when we commit to keeping archives. In selecting archives, organizing them and making them available for use we should always be aware that our goal is to keep these records for ever. This entails a range of management functions and skills which must be in place to protect and preserve the archives, no matter what their age or medium. Preservation management is something everyone in the team, including support staff and volunteers, should be doing. There is an innate tension between most of the work of managing archives – particularly the provision of access – and the preservation goal. But keeping that goal in mind can improve the other areas of our work. For example, assessing preservation requirements as part of the accessioning process ensures that conservation and packaging needs are being logged as part of one handling of the material, thus preventing unnecessary wear and tear. At the same time, management data is being collected to feed into strategy and priority setting for preservation purposes. Figure 5.1 shows the relationship between preservation and the main archival functions discussed in Chapter 4, indicating the archives management activity that both affects and is affected by preservation considerations.

Preservation planning consists of many elements and Table 5.1 gives a brief overview of the separate elements and what they involve, also noting digital record preservation issues.

In all of these areas we are seeking to prevent damage and/or deterioration, minimize damage that cannot be prevented, to treat damaged material and above all to ensure that the archives remain legible and accessible. Preservation is a complicated regime of care and maintenance where we identify what can be done routinely and what needs special attention. If done correctly, it ensures that the archives we have inherited, together with the archives of our own time, will survive for future generations.

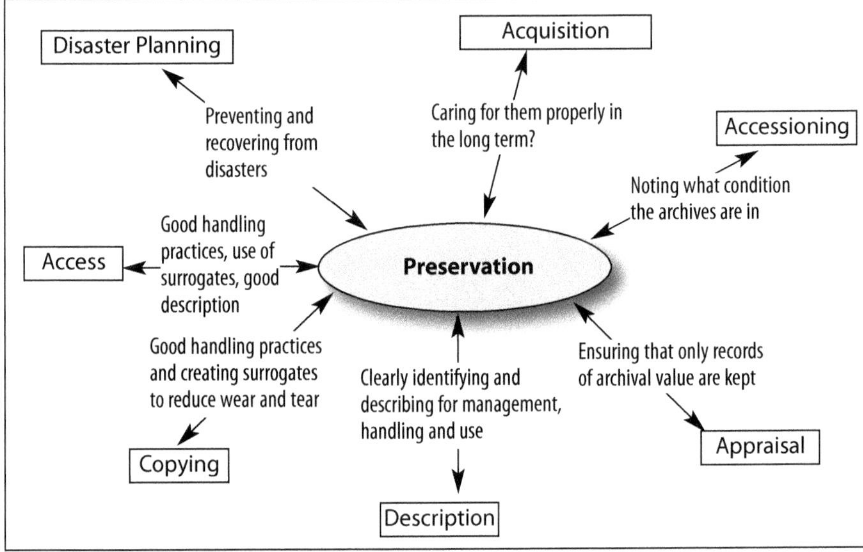

Figure 5.1 *How preservation links to the rest of archives management*

Table 5.1 *Preservation activities overview*

Preservation activity	Physical formats	Digital formats
Creation conditions	Good quality materials with the best chance of physically surviving	As physical **plus** standard formats, open-source programmes
Surveys	Stocktaking, physical assessment, identification of preservation and conservation needs	
Storage environments	Minimal lighting, optimal temperature and humidity for type of media	
Shelving materials	Allowing for safe storage density, resistant to fire, unattractive to pests and mould	As physical **plus** does not conduct magnetic current
Packaging standards	Barrier against elements, resistant to decomposition	
Handling practices	Only when necessary, few items at a time, using great care	
Viewing environments	Minimal lighting, low temperature and humidity, under surveillance	As physical **plus** clean, free from magnetic currents, via access copies if possible
Creation and use of surrogates	For fragile and popular items, and for wider dissemination To protect originals and information contained	
Conservation requirements	Professional expertise to repair damaged items	Digital forensics and archaeology for partial or total reconstruction of software as well as records
Risk management	Identification and reduction or elimination of threats	
Disaster prevention	Prevention or mitigation of threats	
Emergency planning	Preparations to deal with and recover from disasters	

Policy and strategy

A preservation policy is an agreed statement on the repository's aims and strategic approach to preserving archives. As with all policies, it provides the framework rather than the detail of what to do and how. The preservation policy forms part of the overall repository policy and takes account of the aims of the organization, the needs of users and the repository's place in the local and national framework. Preservation management resides in an overall strategy aimed at managing the archives properly in accordance with access goals. All of these factors influence preservation policy. Table 5.2 provides a

Table 5.2 *Preservation policy contents*

Content area	Notes	Example
Purpose/aims	A statement of preservation aims in the context of the repository as a whole	To provide a framework of care for archives, ensuring the repository meets its overall objectives whilst maximizing the effectiveness of preservation activity
Scope	What kind of archives it covers; what areas of activity	Archives in all media, in line with the collecting policy; storage, transport and exhibition of archival materials; access provision; handling guidelines; use of surrogates; disaster planning
Authority	The repository's authority to act in preservation matters	Appointed a place of deposit by The National Archives under s 4 (1) of the Public Records Act 1958
Responsibilities	Specifies particular posts	The Head of Repository has overall responsibility for ensuring all archives in her care are subject to a preservation regime appropriate to their medium. The Head of Preservation has day-to-day responsibility for implementing this policy. He works closely with Heads of Access, Digital Records and Cataloguing to ensure that the policy remains fit for purpose in all areas of the repository. All staff and volunteers have a responsibility to implement and uphold this policy and related procedures.
Related policies	Other Repository policies which have a bearing on preservation work	This policy has been drafted in sympathy with the following repository and institutional policies: • digital records • access • collecting • customer care • environmental.
Principles	Statement of the main principle of preservation policy	The following principles are central to our preservation policy: • preservation considerations are at the heart of all repository work • the repository adopts a risk management approach, seeking to prevent damage to archives • physical intervention is kept to a minimum, with the aim of enabling the copying and/or handling of erstwhile fragile materials • ongoing review of current research and technology to ensure that preservation practice remains effective.
Standards	Reference to the standards adhered to by the repository	The repository follows the applicable storage and preservation, conservation, digital preservation and digital security standards.

suggested list of content for preservation policies, together with an example.

The preservation policy provides the authority for preservation work and guides priorities for resources and activity.

Preservation strategy will depend on the individual repository's circumstances, but a range of considerations will come into play here too. The strategy should be based on an overall picture of the content and preservation status of the holdings (see the section on 'Surveys' below for more about benchmarking conservation and preservation status), combined with the resources available. These will not just be financial, but also include staff skills and time, volunteer capacity and the repository's ability to attract external funding. Usually the main aim is to secure as many items as possible, for example improving a damp storage area to ensure the preservation of a large proportion of the holdings. However, sometimes it is politic to expend resources on the conservation or digitization of a few documents to raise the profile of the archives with stakeholders. Another example of taking a strategic approach to preservation management is in the area of standards. The standards a repository sets for itself must be achievable, but they must be in place and monitored to recognize improvement which represents progress.

Creation conditions

The survival prospects of records and archives depend upon the quality of the physical components or initial software environment, as much as on the future care regime. It stands to reason therefore that the physical media we choose for our records must have the highest potential. For paper this means acid-free and permanent ink that will not harm the paper. For audiovisual materials it is increasingly likely that these will be created in digital formats, so it is important to include them in the digital repository. When creating records in other, less common, physical formats it is important to remember that the fragility or durability of the medium will have a huge impact upon the viability and cost of preservation over time. With digital records the trick is to choose an open format where the coding can be reconstructed and a medium where the lifespan can be accurately predicted.

Surveys

The preservation survey will establish the overall status of preservation in the repository, identify areas of risk or concern, document conservation requirements and set priorities. It will also provide a benchmark to manage progress. The survey should gather information about the amount of material in the various formats and the overall condition of the holdings, as well as any material that is damaged or deteriorating. It is also important to note any existing duplicates or surrogates. The survey allows you to analyse the condition of archive holdings and compliance with preservation good practice and standards. You can then identify the preservation options for each category of record depending on its medium and condition as well as the potential cost. The survey thus needs to investigate not just the holdings but the repository itself. Figure 5.2 provides an example of a survey form.

The survey findings provide the basis for analysis of and recommendations on:

- the archives building(s)
- the general condition of the archive holdings, broken down as appropriate to medium and/or storage, processing or handling space and treatment
- preservation policy, strategy and priorities
- in-house conservation facilities and resources.

As with all aspects of managing records and archives, if you don't know what you have and what issues you face, you cannot begin to manage it. The preservation survey is your primary tool and you will need to periodically update it.

Storage requirements

Storage factors are vital to the preservation of physical and digital formats. In the digital arena IT experts manage the servers in the server rooms, as we depend on conservators to care for physical archives and their storage. In Chapter 3 we noted that archival storage is more stringent in terms of physical environmental factors and security than storage for records that will eventually be destroyed and, again, this goes for all formats.

Essentially, environmental factors, pests, human carelessness and mould cause damage to physical media and speed up the rate of decay. Uncontrolled access risks damage and theft. The speed of technological change and obsolescence pose risks to digital records, including audiovisual ones. Thus we aim to establish an environment which protects the archives from these threats, listed and explained in Table 5.3.

To guard against these threats, the storage space should be in a brick, stone or concrete building and kept dark, cool, dry, well ventilated, pest-free and secure. If there are windows, these should be locked shut and covered to keep out the light, particularly ultra-violet rays. If air conditioning is required, the system should only serve the strong room(s), which should not be included in the heating system for the building. Electrical wires and water pipes should not run through the storage areas. It is best not to store archives in basements

Building, room or space ID			
Preservation element	Status	Relevant standard(s)	Compliance
Location			
Security			
Temperature			
Humidity			
Illumination			
Storage furniture			
Pipes and wiring			
Fire precautions			
Flood precautions			
Housekeeping			
Pest control			
Reading room/access provision			
Preservation element	Status	Relevant standard(s)	Compliance
Location			
Security			
Temperature			
Humidity			
Illumination			
Pipes and wiring			
Fire precautions			
Flood precautions			
Housekeeping			
Pest control			
Furniture			
Access policy and guidance			
Access equipment (supports, etc.)			
Archives management			
Preservation element	Status	Relevant standard(s)	Compliance
Preservation policy (all media)			
Handling guidelines			
Packaging guidelines			
Staff training			
Conservation policy			
Conservation procedures			
Disaster prevention and emergency plan			
Exhibition/loan conditions			

Figure 5.2 *Example of a preservation survey form*

(Continued on facing page)

Holdings					
Location	Catalogue reference	Media/format	Packaging (primary/secondary)	Physical condition*	Digital issues
*note whether in good condition or too fragile to handle, as well as soil or surface dirt and signs of stains or damage					

Figure 5.2 *Continued*

and attics, because these are the areas most vulnerable to damp and, under the roof at least, to heat.

Storage environments

There are many different standards specifying the ideal temperature and humidity for archive storage, depending on the type of media. The two important points to remember are these:

1. Fluctuations in temperature and humidity also cause harm to the archives, and so it is sometimes better to find a temperature and humidity level that can be steadily maintained over time.
2. If you have archives in different media but no possibility of giving them separate storage rooms, you will have to find a compromise on the temperature and humidity, because the optimal levels for digital and audiovisual media are different to those for paper.

Temperature and relative humidity can be measured with a device known as a thermo-hygrograph. Modern technology allows you to collect readings on

Table 5.3 *Threats to archives*

Threat	**Explanation**
Human carelessness and malice	Causes damage, theft and destruction
Insects and rodents	Damage and destroy the media
Heat	Makes the media dry, brittle and unstable
Humidity	Makes paper limp or damp, digital media become unstable
Mould	Prevents archives from being read as well as posing a health risk
Light	Causes chemical changes to occur in paper resulting in discoloration, fading and loss of strength; can damage digital media
Chemicals	Cause a negative reaction in archival media
Obsolescence	Causes illegibility

a small data logger which downloads into a programme to provide statistics over time. You need equipment to measure the environment regularly in different parts of your storage spaces and record it over time. This will provide you with reassurance that the conditions are right for preserving the archives and, if not, with the evidence for resources to correct the situation.

Modern building practices and techniques, with their emphasis on low environmental impact, chime well with archive storage requirements, since use of technology and engineering to maintain the optimum temperature and humidity are prone to periods where the target readings are not met. If the building itself is built to be thermally neutral, not only will the internal environment be more stable and environmentally friendly, it will also be less expensive to run. The recently opened French National Archives building on the outskirts of Paris is a good example of this. Research showed that 30-centimetre thick concrete walls were the best option for storage areas.

On a more practical note, it is more space-efficient to have a large storage area than several small ones and entrances need to be easy to negotiate with a trolley. It follows that if the storage areas are above or below ground level, an elevator will probably be necessary.

Security

For records of all media, good security is crucial. It is a basic principle of archives management that the guarantee of unbroken custody and safeguarding against unauthorized access contribute to the reliability of the records – and this is even more true in the digital arena. The storage area should be self-contained and only used for archival material. All doors and windows should be kept securely locked and access limited to archives staff. If access has to be granted to others, maintenance personnel for example, they should be accompanied at all times.

Shelving

We keep archives on shelves for many reasons, but the main ones are:

- to keep them off the floor and out of standing water in the event of a flood (the bottom shelf should always be 6 inches (15 cm) off the ground).
- to manage the density at which they are packed and stacked to reduce stress and compression and to ensure good airflows.
- to allow easy, damage-free placement and removal of boxes.
- so the top shelf can act as roof protection against water and other hazards from above.

We use metal shelving because it is not as vulnerable to fire as wood, does not attract pests or give off chemicals. It is also stronger and lighter, which is particularly important if you go for mobile shelving to make the best use of available space. If shelving is not available boxes can be placed on pallets as a temporary solution pending a move.

Housekeeping

An important aspect of preservation is housekeeping, particularly in the storage areas. Cleaning will be necessary but bringing water in risks raising the relative humidity, so dry methods are best. Also, cleaners who are not part of the staff are both a security and a physical risk, particularly contractors which may have a high staff turnover. Regular cleaning and regular security checks provide the side benefit of a human being walking the premises on a regular basis. Because they know how things look, feel and smell, they will be able to detect if something is a bit 'off', perhaps a smell that indicates a leak, or something out of place which has been mis-shelved.

Pests

Insects and rodents eat paper, parchment and book bindings and use them to make their homes. There are a number of things that can be done to protect against them, as set out in Checklist 5.1.

Checklist 5.1 Measures for protection against pests

- Keeping the storage areas clean, as detailed in the Housekeeping section
- Thoroughly checking all records when they are brought into the archives and dealing with any infestation before they can contaminate the storage area
- Regular inspections of the storage area for signs of pests such as dead insects, rodent droppings, shredded paper or powder resulting from the boring activities of insects
- Use of insect and rodent traps to monitor the presence and location of pests
- Never consuming food in the storage area, keeping the surrounding areas clear of waste food.

If you discover insect infestation or rodent activity, isolate and remove the affected records and call in experts. Remember that they may need to be briefed on the special requirements for archives.

Packaging, handling and access

Packaging

Archives need to be packaged whenever possible, even volumes where the binding will provide a measure of protection to the contents. There are two levels of packaging: primary, which is mandatory and should be a box, and secondary, which is ideal and may be a wrap, a clear sleeve or a folder, depending on the item. Boxes provide a first line of defence against many of the hazards that may affect archives, such as fire, water, dirt and dust, insects and rodents and atmospheric fluctuations. Even if you cannot budget for archival-quality boxes for all your holdings at once, putting all holdings in the highest-quality box you can afford will be a positive preservation measure.

Archival standard packaging materials for paper are pH neutral (neither acidic nor alkaline), lest they affect the acidity of the paper. Since boxes made from pH neutral pulp are inherently long-lasting, we use them for all archival media. Archive boxes should not be too large, so they can be easily handled without risk of dropping or shaking. Archival packaging also protects material from damage, particularly during transport; it stabilizes fragile material; and, perhaps most importantly, it demonstrates to stakeholders how special archives are and that we must treat them carefully and package them properly, thus encouraging the same respect from others. Table 5.4 gives recommendations for packaging for the main types of archive formats.

Table 5.4 *Packaging recommendations*

Archives	Packaging
Paper	Acid-neutral folders and acid-neutral boxes – staples and rivets must be non-rusting
Photographic prints	Clear inert polyester envelopes, stored in metal cabinets or archival standard boxes
Magnetic tape	Keep in original container in a soft polyethylene bag, in archival standard boxes, protected from magnetic fields
CDs, DVDs, digital media	Keep in original cases or purpose-designed packaging in archival standard boxes, protected from magnetic fields
Maps and large format records	Store flat in acid-free board portfolios or rolled around acid-neutral cylinders and wrapped in archival quality material

When deciding and selecting archival quality packaging it is sensible to find some basic items which will serve for almost all your holdings, for example:

- a standard repository box of a size that fits on your shelves in a space-efficient manner (if you need larger or smaller boxes, make them half- or double-size to optimize the space)
- folders which fit into the boxes
- inert plastic sleeves that fit into the folders and boxes.

For large or awkwardly shaped items it is possible to procure tailor-made acid-neutral packaging but if you want to save time and money you can easily adapt existing materials. Boxes can be padded out with archival tissue paper for smaller items and acid-neutral paper and card can be used to wrap and construct boxes. Remember that archives of different sizes and formats do not have to be stored together physically even if they are from the same creator, as long as the finding aids maintain the connection between physically separated records. This makes the best use of space as well as protecting the archives.

Boxes should not be too densely packed and there should be space for ventilation within the box, as well as for fingers to extract the records. Documents should be kept flat wherever possible but, if kept upright, 'spacers' or supports should be used to prevent folders slipping down inside partially filled boxes. Preparing documents for packing also allows some basic preservation measures to be taken, such as removing metal fasteners which tend to rust, perished rubber bands and dried-out pressure tape. Use brass or plastic paper clips or folders to keep papers together.

Handling

The best preservation strategy is one that keeps the records in a sort of stasis according to the standards described in the preceding sections. It is the great tension of archives management goals that our aim to preserve the material for ever is at odds with our aim to make the contents available to our stakeholders. The sad fact is that the archives are at most risk when they are handled by human beings, staff and researchers alike. The only protection we can give the archives is to ensure that all of us handle them with respect and care. If records look as if they are cared for, for example packaged well, then people will handle them with care.

Checklist 5.2 gives comprehensive handling guidelines that can be tailored to the use of staff, volunteers or researchers.

Checklist 5.2 Handling guidelines

We are keeping the archives to make the information and evidence they contain available not just to us but to future generations. Because they are unique and cannot be replaced if they are damaged, it is vitally important that we handle them with care according to these guidelines:

- Always handle archives carefully, ensuring that your hands are clean and free of creams/moisturizers and keeping contact to a minimum.
- Don't pick single papers up by their corners – slide a hand underneath to support them.

- Always carry archives in a box. Do not carry more than two boxes together – use a trolley and ladders to access and carry archive boxes.
- If transporting archives outside, make sure the boxes are covered.
- Don't pick up volumes by their spines and always use two hands when removing heavy volumes from the shelf.
- Don't turn pages by flicking the top corner or by licking your fingers.
- Photographs should be sleeved before handling. Hold them by the edges to avoid skin contact when sleeving them.
- Don't lean on documents, either to keep them flat or to make notes.
- Don't place other objects on records.
- Don't crowd too many items onto the work surface.
- Don't eat or drink around the archives.
- Always use pencil, not ink, when consulting the archives.
- Support heavy or fragile items during use with the equipment provided.
- Cotton gloves may need to be used for handling original photographs and audiovisual materials, but not for all materials, as this reduces dexterity.
- When filming or copying records take extra care in handling them – do not press, fold or bend, or allow them to get hot from the process.

Access

Although we discussed providing access to archives thoroughly in Chapter 4, it is important to consider reading rooms from the perspective of preservation. Access provision should include the withdrawal of material which is at risk. Although the risk of theft is not high, the following precautions should be taken:

- ensure that a member of staff is supervising users and they are not left alone with archives
- keep a record of what records each researcher consults
- fix a maximum number of items that may be consulted at one time
- do not allow bags or other containers into the research area.

Creation and use of surrogates

Surrogate: a copy of an archive used as a replacement in order to preserve the original or offer increased access. May be to a like-to-like medium or to a different medium or format.

Archivists have always used surrogates as part of preservation management.

For example, microfilm was used extensively in archives for large record series that were very popular with researchers, particularly birth, marriage and death registers, to save wear and tear on the originals. It is worth noting, though, that microfilm or fiche also wears out, although if not used and if kept at the right temperature and humidity it can last for a very long time. Another area where surrogates are important is in managing audiovisual archives. It is good practice to keep the original in the correct storage environment once two copies have been made: one to take more copies from when required and one for access. A surrogate can also be a paper copy of an archive document made on a photocopy machine.

Computer technology has increasingly made possible the creation of digital images of archives, both to preserve them and to provide much greater access than was possible before. It is now common to place images of archival material on websites where they can be viewed by people across the globe, also allowing many people to view the same record at the same time. In creating digital surrogates of textual records, we have the possibility of adding full-text searching using optical character recognition functionality, although its archival description metadata remains invaluable for providing context and allowing more global searching across the repository's holdings and beyond. With digital images in particular it is useful to be able to make and keep a high-resolution image whilst also having lower-resolution images to provide access or copies to researchers. Another reason for providing copies is to facilitate access to large, unwieldy items which are either difficult to access or at risk of damage if accessed. Surrogates are also used in vital record protection strategies in case a disaster takes out the originals – either permanently or temporarily. Disaster prevention and emergency planning is discussed in the next section.

Whilst it is possible to create surrogates on demand, it is better to have a policy and to do it in a planned way. Researchers can be resistant to using copies, particularly microfiche, and there needs to be a clear statement about the purpose of the surrogacy programme and when it is appropriate to allow someone to view the original – for example, if it has inherent information such as a watermark that cannot be seen in the copy. The policy will indicate which records are a priority for copying and in which media and format they should be created.

Above all, it is vital to ensure that surrogacy creation is carried out to very high standards, as follows:

- Original records are handled carefully according to articulated guidelines, especially when being filmed or copied.
- Copies should be accurately mapped to the originals and their finding aids, via physical labels and adequate metadata, depending on the surrogacy media.

- Copies should be quality-controlled to ensure that the images are good and clear and the metadata requirements have been met.
- A long-term preservation strategy is in place to ensure that copies remain accessible for as long as possible and additional copies can be made (preferably without recourse to the original again) if required.

Disaster prevention and emergency planning

Since archives are unique and irreplaceable, disasters such as fire or flood can have a devastating effect. Financial insurance to repair buildings and replace shelving, packaging and equipment that has been damaged, as well as to repair and conserve damaged archives, is important but because they are irreplaceable, it is not the only protection that archives need against such threats. The best protection is a thorough risk evaluation, a good comprehensive programme to prevent risks from materializing, a plan of what to do in the event of any kind of disaster and ensuring that all staff are well trained in emergency recovery procedures. If you do this you will ensure that many risks are averted or reduced. If the worst happens, you won't waste time deciding what to do, searching for supplies and training people to help, which means you can immediately focus your resources on recovery.

Disaster prevention

The first step in developing a disaster plan is to analyse the risks and threats. We have already discussed many of the common and constant threats to archives, such as mould and pests and ways of avoiding or reducing them, which we expect to live with on a daily basis. Table 5.5 provides a list of the more catastrophic risks which are perhaps less likely to happen but which we should be prepared for, together with mitigation actions.

Table 5.5 *Risk mitigation*

Risk	Action
Building or equipment failure or malfunction, resulting in fire, flood, crushed/damaged archives	Keep buildings in good repair, maintain equipment and test electrical wiring regularly, monitor temperature and humidity, inspect routinely
Force of nature (volcanic eruptions, earthquakes, tornados, etc.), resulting in fire, flood, crushed/damaged/destroyed/lost archives	Ensure that building meets recommended specifications to withstand event, have evacuation plan and vital records programme for archives
Deliberate malfeasance (theft, vandalism, terrorism, etc.) resulting in fire, flood, damaged/destroyed/stolen archives	Good security, staff awareness, join a local disaster plan network
Human error (unlocked door, smouldering cigarette, careless computer key stroke) resulting in fire, flood, damaged/lost archives	Regular staff training, adequate supervision, constant awareness

Developing the emergency plan

Disaster prevention and recovery is an organization-wide responsibility, not just one that is important for archives to manage. If the archives are part of a wider organization it is important to liaise with colleagues concerned with the organizational disaster plan. Even if the archives *are* the organization, you will need to establish links with local fire, flood and security agencies to be informed about the services they can offer, to tap into their expertise and to ensure that they are aware of the special requirements for archives.

Once you have created a list of the potential risks to the archives and identified ongoing prevention and mitigation actions for each of them, you can plan what to do in the event that a disaster strikes. Obviously, for many of these risks there will also be a scale of possible effect: a fire might burn all of the holdings, or only a small proportion; similarly, a flood might soak everything or just records stored below the height to which the water has risen, or higher humidity levels cause mould. Therefore you should anticipate the broad range of disaster scenarios and map out the action you would need to take for each of them. In many cases the action will be similar, just to a greater or lesser extent, or requiring a slightly different set of skills. When you have this master list of disaster scenarios and recovery actions you can list the skills, equipment and other resources you would need to implement the plan in the event of disaster. The emergency plan should include the points shown in Checklist 5.3.

Checklist 5.3 Elements of an emergency plan

- Training of staff and volunteers both on a regular basis and a quick refresher in the event of an emergency
- Establishing and maintaining reciprocal links with neighbouring archive repositories and other individuals and organizations that could assist
- Stocking supplies (possibly stored off-site) for the recovery effort, such as plastic crates, gloves, overalls, tools, packing materials
- Responsibilities in case of an emergency, including responsibility for declaring one and deciding which resources, staff and action is needed
- Up-to-date staff list and contact details, together with contact details for emergency services and other individuals and organizations who might help
- A description of each anticipated emergency scenario and the point at which an emergency should be declared
- Procedures for ascertaining that the situation is stable and the buildings are safe
- Priorities for recovery (e.g., records in more vulnerable media, records on loan to the archives).
- Procedures for removing damaged or at-risk archives from storage areas

- Provision for freeze-drying wet archives and/or drying them out, procedures for staff
- Provision for temporary storage of archives
- Procedures for handling the anticipated range of damaged items, including tracking archive references and metadata
- Actions to be taken to restore the storage areas, responsibility for declaring return to normal
- Procedures for replacing all material and updating location registers and finding aids.

The plan needs to be kept up to date and all staff and volunteers should be aware of it and their role in the event of a disaster. Key staff should keep a copy of the plan at home – it is no use having it in an office that is inaccessible because of the emergency.

We covered vital records identification and protection in Chapter 3, and so we do not need to repeat it here, but bear in mind that, although not necessarily business-critical, all archives are vital. They have been carefully selected to provide the permanent record of the organization or aspect of human activity the archives seek to document, but it is rarely possible to create security copies of everything. There are some archives management records that are vital – for example, the accessions register, finding aids, the location register and plans of the storage area – and these should be copied and kept where they can be available immediately in an emergency.

Disaster recovery

The initial and main benefit of having a disaster plan is that it provides a protocol to follow at a time when staff and management alike will be suffering from shock and possibly less able to plan and prioritize. It will guide decisions on who to contact (perhaps not everyone will be needed at once), what action to take and where to get additional support and resources.

The emergency plan will kick in once an emergency has been declared, possibly before it is possible to go back into the premises, and it marks the point at which you can begin to recover from the disaster. Remember that the most important thing is to protect human lives and prevent harm and injury, so ensure that no one goes back into the premises before the emergency services have declared it is safe to do so. It will also be important to ensure that everyone wears appropriate protective clothing and takes regular breaks – the work will be physically demanding and it will also be naturally distressing to see the archives in such poor shape, so it is important to keep up staff morale.

It can be a long road to recovery. The building housing the Cologne City

Archives collapsed in 2009 and in 2013 the holdings were still temporarily housed in archive storage facilities around Germany, including the Federal Archives in Berlin, which had frozen waterlogged records in its freezers. However, it is vital to take quick action in the event of a disaster, to stabilize the situation and prevent things getting worse – mould will occur within a couple of days if the archives are damp and the temperature rises! It is not possible to go into all of the detail of how to treat damaged archives in this book, but a good disaster plan will include procedures to cover any scenario and provide for staff and volunteer training.

Once things are back to normal and the effects of the disaster have been mitigated as much as possible it is important to review the plan and the emergency response activity. This is not to find fault but rather a chance to identify and credit good work and to improve the plan and procedures in future.

Moving archives

Archives are very vulnerable if they need to be moved, for example to a new storage area or repository. The risk is that they will be damaged or lost during the move. It is important to plan any move carefully, to ensure that security is tight and that the holdings are carefully packed and wrapped for removal. Checklist 5.4 provides guidance on moving archives.

Checklist 5.4 Archives removals

Do

- brief removal company on special requirements for archives.
- use pallets to keep archives off the ground and track groups of material.
- check box contents will not move.
- shrink or bubble-wrap volumes.
- have clear procedure to track items off shelves onto new shelf.

Don't

- move without insurance to cover conservation work if archives get damaged.
- leave storage areas unsecured at any time.
- stack boxes too high (bottom ones can get crushed).
- leave boxes stacked for long.
- leave transport vehicles unsecured at any time.

Exhibitions

Although it poses a risk to archives, it is sometimes desirable to use original records in exhibitions. The risks are the same as any in use of archives: changes in temperature and humidity, exposure to high levels of light, damage and theft. Depending on the kind of exhibition, the archives may be on loan to another organization, in which case a stringent loan agreement must be in place. The basic points to bear in mind are set out in Checklist 5.5.

Checklist 5.5 Guidelines for exhibiting archive material

- Damaged or fragile items should not be displayed or loaned.
- Check the archives' condition and conserve if necessary.
- Security must be high at all times, including storage, transport and display.
- The conditions in the display cases must meet the relevant standards for environment and light.
- Exhibited material should be supported.
- A record of the archives' movements and display conditions must be created and kept indefinitely.
- Nothing should ever be kept on permanent display.
- Any loan agreement should include standards for handling, storage and exhibition as well as indemnity against damage.
- A member of staff should accompany loaned items.

Conservation requirements

Conservation: the area of expertise concerned with repairing and strengthening damaged and fragile archival materials such that they can be safely handled.

Conservation is a discrete area of expertise and conservation professionals usually work alongside archivists to provide advice and carry out the function of physically repairing, strengthening and packaging archives so as to protect them and prevent damage. If you do not have a conservator on staff it is a good idea to identify sources of conservation expertise in case you need it, as well as to be clear about the terms of any contracted work. It is also possible that you can learn to carry out some aspects of conservation work yourself, for example dry-cleaning or minor repair work.

It is very costly to conserve records, so it is important to be strategic in deciding how to treat damaged or fragile records. It may be better to copy them and keep them securely in stable conditions whilst the surrogate provides access to the information. It is important that conservation is included in the overall preservation policy and that it covers priorities, procedures and materials. You – or the conservation staff – should always keep a record of work done to any record.

Preservation of digital records

Although this book tries to integrate all aspects of managing records and archives in all media, there are some special conditions around the long-term preservation of digital records which have been designated as archives. It is an area of expertise which is quite specialized and often practised by people with IT, not archives, backgrounds. It is therefore crucial that we understand the challenges to and principles of effective digital preservation strategies in order to be able to manage preservation for all of our holdings.

The challenges

Digital records are quite complex in terms of their physical makeup. In essence they consist of the medium and the text or record information in binary code, with additional metadata, also in binary form, about the file format and delineation of the various records where more than one is on the same media unit (the file structure). So far so good, but the medium, be it CD, magnetic tape or hard drive, requires hardware, software, an operating system and power to read the record. All of these are subject to deterioration but the software and hardware is also subject to obsolescence as new technology supersedes it and is used to create records. The result is that within a relatively short space of time the records may not be accessible, because the software is unavailable, there is no hardware left to accommodate the medium type or the medium itself has deteriorated.

A second challenge to preserving digital records has to do with some long-held principles about managing archives, one of which is that the record should not be changed, or it either becomes a different record or its credibility is compromised. It can be almost impossible to identify the original record when it is created in a computer system, as almost immediately back-up records are created, not to mention multimedia records and records that come together from various sources to deliver a report which records the state of play at a given time. In the longer term, in order to preserve digital records we need to change them – either to transfer them from one medium to another or to convert them from an obsolete format to one that is current. This has involved a paradigm shift from the traditional archival principles, but those principles have helped to ensure that we have standards and practices to retain the integrity and reliability of digital records.

Digital preservation strategy

Since digital records preservation is in its infancy and there are no solutions which have been tried and tested over any length of time, the best way to approach it is with a strategy that aims to ensure that the content and evidence in the records remains legible and there is metadata to provide reassurance that the records are what they purport to be, including providing an audit trail of preservation measures. In a way this is analogous to conserving paper archives. The conservator repairs the record such that it is strengthened and usable but in such a way that it is obvious it has been repaired. Your preservation strategy must include:

- keeping the original data as evidence of records that have been changed to ensure their preservation
- checking records regularly to ensure that they are still legible
- copying onto new media when existing media reaches end of life
- choosing standard and open file formats
- migrating to new file formats before old ones become obsolete
- using standards for all aspects of digital archives management
- capturing and managing descriptive, technological and preservation metadata.

A great deal of digital preservation research is going on, not just in the archives and records management field but also in libraries and all areas where digital data is created, collected and kept for any length of time. Keeping informed about developments is a crucial part of your strategy. You should also be familiar with the main standards used in digital preservation. The most important ones are the ones specifying the requirements for digital repositories:

1 ISO 16363:2012 *Space Data and Information Transfer Systems – Audit and Certification of Trustworthy Digital Repositories*
2 ISO 14721:2003 Space Data and Information Transfer Systems – Open Archival Information System – Reference Model.

Digital repositories

The digital repository plays a crucial role in digital preservation and just as the physical repository is more than the building and shelving, the digital equivalent is more than hardware and software. It includes:

- secure digital storage
- software to manage records and metadata (ideally open-format, so that

the records and their metadata can be migrated if necessary at any time without loss of data or links)
- policy and procedures for managing the repository and the records
- a maintained list of acceptable file formats: open-source file formats are best because they tend to be more stable and the programming is freely available and easier to reproduce to access records in old formats
- content control and management
- ongoing regime of technology maintenance and upgrades
- metadata selection, creation and maintenance according to a specified metadata schema, including automatic and manually added metadata. The main types of metadata to consider are:
  - preservation (current and past record formats)
  - security (audit trails, fixity algorithms[1])
  - description
  - technical (file size, page count, encryption)
  - structural (inter-relationships between files)
  - access rights
- back-up and/or replication site in case of disaster or temporary outage
- workflow (a series of tasks to manage the records) as follows:
  - transfer to temporary storage area for checking
  - virus check
  - check or add digital fingerprint
  - check all metadata is present
  - check content
  - determine format and validate against published specification, change if necessary
  - document the records' size, resolution, compression, number of pages, embedded video or objects, password protection information
  - transfer to digital repository to store files and metadata
  - delete records from transfer area
  - create access copies
  - activate audit trails
  - preservation management (checking still readable, batch migration with documentation).

Round-up

As we have seen, archival preservation affects all areas of archive work. It aims at an all-encompassing environment of care, regardless of where the archives are (in the strong room, on a server, in transit, in the reading room, on a photocopier, in the hands of staff or on display). It should be a common culture and approach for the repository, every member of staff and all researchers to ensure that the archives have the best possible chance of surviving into the future.

Note

1 Fixity algorithms provide a way of checking that the record has not been changed, as they give a value that can only come from that record.

Conclusion

Records management is crucial to ensuring that any organization can perform its mission effectively and can demonstrate transparency and accountability to its stakeholders; archives management ensures that we have reliable recorded evidence of the history of individuals, organizations and society as a whole. This book has followed the record's path from creation in an adequate recordkeeping system, through the application of classification and access techniques, evaluation for business, legal and historical value to proper destruction or preservation and access in the archive. Regardless of whether the cycle is split into two separate functions within an organization, the two are inextricably linked and complement each other.

Select bibliography

Bettington, J., Eberhard, K., Loo, R. and Smith, C. (eds) (2008) *Keeping Archives*, 3rd edn, Australian Society of Archivists, Inc.

Forde, H. and Rhys-Lewis, J. (2013) *Preserving Archives*, 2nd edn, Facet Publishing.

Hamer, A. (2011) *The ICSA Guide to Document Retention*, 3rd edn, ICSA Publishing.

Millar, L. (2010) *Archives: principles and practices*, Facet Publishing.

Index